"YOU WILL NEVER HEAR I TOLD YOU SO FROM JESUS."

"I TOLD YOU SO"

THIS BOOK IS THE BIBLE OF LIFE

JERRY MANUKIN

ISBN 979-8-89428-236-7 (paperback)
ISBN 979-8-89428-237-4 (hardcover)
ISBN 979-8-89428-238-1 (digital)

Christian Faith Publishing
832 Park Avenue
Meadville, PA 16335
www.christianfaithpublishing.com

Printed in the United States of America

Contents

A Sure Bet

At one time or another, we gamble. It could be sports or card games or horses or your life. We convince ourselves it's just for fun. Who do we think we're kidding? Most of the time, it is out of desperation. We sometimes spend way too much on not a sure thing. We may be on a path where we need fast money. So with what little we have, we play the lottery. Or some other way to make quick money. We may get lucky and win some money, so we bet a little more, thinking, "I will keep on winning." So sad. We are not gullible, nor are we stupid for doing so. We are just grasping at straws. Keep playing; you have Satan on your side. With that said, you should never give up hope. No, I don't mean gambling, and you will win. Satan likes to throw you a bone. Odds of winning are against you. And when you run out of cash, and you spend your hard-earned money, we say, "Oh, it was just for fun." Remember that excuse is just for you. Sorry to upset you; Satan loves it. Why don't we bet on a sure thing! Simply ask Jesus to help you out of this dilemma, as Jesus is the only sure bet. Not only will your life be on the right path, your mind and your health will approve tremendously as well. You must be patient and pray to our God. You will find out in a very short time you are on the path that God laid out for you and where Satan will never go. Just ask God for forgiveness and confess your sins. You will never lose with Jesus; that's a sure bet.

In my lifetime, God gave me only what I needed, nothing more, and if he gave me more and I didn't realize it, I must have given it to you.

Adversity

I believe we all want things to go well: we pray for all good things to happen. We sometimes go out of our way to help others, especially in believing in God. We should learn when to back off and let God take the lead. We cannot accomplish everything by ourselves. I know we would like to, but sometimes, that is an impossible task. That is when we should go into God's world spiritually. We should not wait until it is too late to ask for help, for ourselves and others. We cannot control adversity, nor should we let adversity control us. Stay strong, and be fearless. Do not let your mind go into a negative mode. That just adds to adversity and is making any situation much worse (in our minds). Sometimes, when things go awry, I try to smile and think of the good things in life. You should control your mind. That is where the heart and God steps in. We can and will overcome all adversities.

(Please, God, let my faults be limited and
protect me and all that is close to me.)

It works for all that is pure of heart.
Now is better than never.

Amazing

If I had a penny for every thought you have throughout the day and night, I would be a wealthy man. Let's give you another thought and me another penny. I ask why, why, why do you think so much? You should not worry about the future, and you most assuredly should forget the past, so where does that leave you? That answer is easy because the only thing left is today, now, and this moment. With that said, it is a good thing to think about today, but it is a bad thing to dwell on it. I know we sometimes would like the world to just stop and keep all the happy days and all the good things in life. Don't give up on that thought because it is not a dream. It may happen. When you close your eyes, say a prayer for Jesus. His world stopped. And he kept going for all eternity, and so can you. Not to worry, don't weaken your body with stress. God has you covered. Just go about your daily habits. If you need a hobby or a stress reliever, learn to hum. You won't be embarrassed if someone walked in on you. They would probably join you in humming. Isn't that a lovely thought and a beautiful picture to remember? This *new you* will happen, maybe not in a day or two, but very shortly. Remember, God created his world in six days, and even he had to rest.

This letter is a message from Jesus personally to you from his father.

Make a wish.

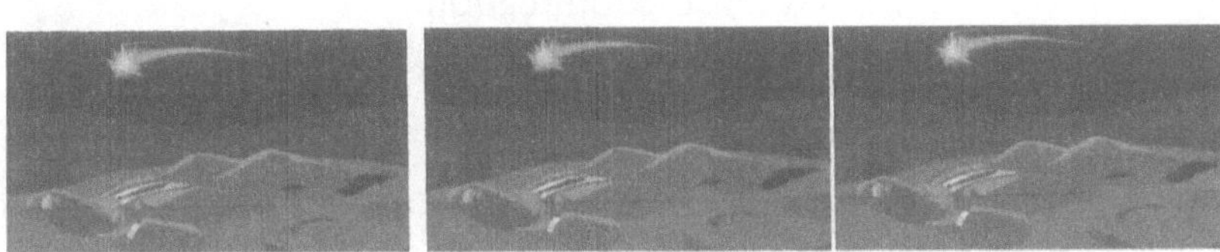

Answers

We spend way too much time looking for answers. We seem to be troubled, but we don't know why. We are looking for answers. An event just does not go how we planned it. We worked so hard to get everything the way we thought it should be to make it successful. Unfortunately, it did not turn out the way you expected it to. Still looking for answers. I woke up this morning with a smile on my face and was very cheerful, thinking nothing was going to ruin my happy face or change my smile to a frown. Guess what? Yes, you guessed it. Still looking for answers. Even though I don't have the answers to all that I go through in my life (still looking for answers). I do know where I can find all the answers I am looking for; it's like shopping for what you want in one place. That place is in God's house. He has the answers to all your questions. He has the answers to your love questions when a relationship just does not work out. He has the answers for your workplace when you are being given a hard time when you feel you're doing your best. He has the answers to all your health issues. He has the answer to your people's problems. The best part of all this is you only have to ask. The only cost of this service from God is your loyalty to him. Dear Jesus, I try very hard at what I do. Please make my endeavors successful. Put that smile back on my face. Also, Jesus, don't make this temporary; make this permanent. Thank you, Jesus, I love you.

God is the foundation.
You are the building.

At Last

We live every day of our lives wondering about tomorrow. And most of the time, thinking about yesterday. Let those times, the past, and the future be what they are—past and future, especially the past; and if we don't, we will miss some of the future. We should try to live our life for today. Tomorrow will come fast enough. We should concentrate on bettering our lives and the lives of others and hope they (the others) will do the same for us. I don't presume to think that I know what is in store for me. I only ask Jesus to give me some hints on how my life is going, keep me updated on my progress in his paradise, and also give me the wisdom and strength to help myself. I mean both mentally and physically. I know I can do anything (with God's help). Sometimes I feel so alone even when I'm with someone. *It's not you; it's me.* And at some point, we should just stop thinking. And one day, I hope in the near future I can say at last I understand myself.

Jesus understands my life.
It works for all that is pure of heart.
Now is better than never.

Attraction

At a very young age, even as young as five years old we are attracted to someone. Why is that? Why do we seem to enjoy being around some and not others? That seems to happen all our life. We pick certain people to be our friends, and we ignore others or at least we try. Why is that? As we reach our teens, we seem to turn our attraction to a single person who seems interesting to us more than anyone else. Why is that? We meet our so-called one and only, especially in our minds. And for some reason, we are locked into that single relationship. For now. Now is where we have to be very careful, as God may be sending you this person or Satan may be. If at any time you feel pressured or bullied by this individual, whether it be male or female, don't walk away from this relationship. Run as fast as you can and end this. Now we know Satan had a hand in this, and God gave you the wisdom to end this relationship, God will send you someone that you will, without a doubt, feel the warmth and love in your heart and mind and do not look back and be reminded of the past, and if you committed a sin with that other person, confess what it was to God and ask for forgiveness and move on. You do not have to waste your precious life as if you are walking on eggs. Your new relationship is now on course, and you are smiling more. PS: Your closest friends will know the difference in your demeanor. And God can concentrate on others now that you are safe.

Make sure the voice you hear is God's.

Baby Steps

Life begins when we take our first step (baby steps if you will). We are so eager to use our new talent to discover everything around us. We are on shaky ground until we get the knack of it. We eventually build up our bravery and balance. So now we think we are in charge of where we go and what we do. Not so. It is your parents or guardian to guide you. Oh, you try to do this on your own and think, "Hey, I can go anywhere I choose." Again, not so, and if you have caring parents: and/or guardians, they will make you understand this. Like it or not, they are the leaders and your protector. Are you listening, parents? Parents must remember to be the leader of their children at their first steps. Oh yes, it's cute, and they do funny things, and we think some things are funny, and they are, but be careful how you come across to your child. Because they have their eyes on you. Enough about the little ones. Let's talk about the parents' baby steps, and this has nothing to do with walking. It has to be about teaching your children to be Christians at that age. Not only will you be teaching them about our God, but you will also be surprised at how much you can learn from them. Just remember they are the child, and you are the parent. Also, I don't know all the answers, but I do know who does. And when I seek answers and I am puzzled about what to do, I turn to Jesus. The good thing about that is he is very easy to reach 24-7. All I have to do is reach out to him for answers. He has never failed me. Thank you, Jesus, for my children and teach me to be a loving and caring parent.

We must always mix our yes's and no's to our
children and when to know the difference.

Begging

Why do we feel like we have to beg for things that we want? We are humiliating ourselves by begging, especially when most things we are asking for should rightfully belong to us. Who are we begging for? Are we asking our friends or family for things probably, and that is just distancing us from them. They eventually shy away from us. I believe that begging for food is the only legitimate thing to ask for, as no one in this United States should go hungry. In the days of old, we were able to grow our vegetables and hunt for food. That realization and ability to do that seems to be lost. A tradition most families had when I was growing up. That was a proud time in my life as I knew I could live off the land. Rules and regulations changed my world, but I follow them. So sad our leaders aren't very good leaders; they are good people, but they are followers. Please, God, I beg of you to help me to help them!

Somebody does know your thoughts.
It works for all that is pure of heart.
Now is better than never.

Believe It or Not

Most people believe in something or someone. What is hard to understand? Is it true? People say things they hear from other people, and eventually, it reaches your ears. And a lot of the time, we repeat that to someone else. Believe me, it does not always make it the truth because even if you did not start it, you passed it on. Let's try not to do that because it makes us almost as bad as the one who started the rumor. Now the serious believe it or not. Can you live two lives? The answer is yes. I will explain my theory about this. We sometimes make a pact with the devil and still believe in our God. Do you believe that? Well, sometimes when you go off the deep end and do not believe in Jesus, and when you do, things seem to go better. And you accept that and believe it just happened even when you lost faith. It did not. Satan gave you what you wanted, and you accepted that. This may go on for years before you realize it was not God's will. You should know that because when you did what you were not supposed to, you seemed happy over that. Wrong is wrong. Also, all the days or months or years your pact with Satan seemed to give you power over others. For example, you may be able to smell death even before it happens. Or other unnatural things that you thought were good. It was not, so when you wake up and realize you are on the wrong path, go back to God, and you will feel so free and not feel so guilty. God could have stopped you, but he wants you to live your life. He also wants you to live your life through him and not through Satan. Remember, when you get to heaven, God is the decider, not Satan.

Believe the Unbelievable

Why is it so hard to believe what you did not see? Probably because so many people have misled you, and you don't know who or what to believe. Let your faith take the place of the unbelievable. We must now go with God's motives. He will never lead you astray. It's so hard to just accept some things. A lot of faith and trust in God will tell you when to believe the unbelievable. As an example, when Mary became with child before Mary and Joseph were married, Joseph did not believe Mary when she told him she was never with another man, and yet she was with child. Joseph, in his unbelievable state, turned Mary away. Joseph loved Mary so much he was tormented over this. When Joseph wept himself to sleep, he heard a voice telling him Mary was honest with him. Then Joseph, the God-fearing man, accepted what he heard from God. He was told Mary's child was a child of God. She was carrying Jesus, and Joseph and Mary married, and Joseph's faith was so strong that this doubt was never mentioned again. God created Jesus so he (Jesus) had the power to convince people to be Christians—hence, Jesus's last name (Christ). In a few years, Jesus did just that (made Christians out of nonbelievers—not all, but most. God will send Jesus out to do his (God's) work on Earth. Jesus is now twelve years of age and was being bullied by the locals. Joseph and Mary thought that it was because of this that they could not find him. It was not because of the bullying that Jesus could not be found. I will explain why. Mary and Joseph began to look and asked around if anyone saw him; someone said he went to the chapel. Mary and Joseph went to the chapel and saw Jesus talking to an elder. Joseph began to scold Jesus for going away and not telling them where he was. Jesus said to Joseph, "I did tell you where I was going through one of the people back there. Did he not tell you I was going to my father's house?" Need I say more? Well, I am. Jesus is now eighteen when he left to do God's work.

Amen to all of the above.
If you're the problem, Jesus is the solution.
I don't understand because I'm not part of your world.
So you think you have a busy day?
It works for all that is pure of heart.
Now is better than never.

Black Sheep

Why do we seem to be left out of most family functions? We try to fit in. We are very conscientious of all people, but we still never get invited. Why is that? It seems it is that way with religion as well. It may be that we are too quiet and do not spout off as many others do. I like them but not enough to invite them to my outings because they are embarrassing to me. Maybe my problem, thinking the way I do, when I should look in a mirror, maybe I will understand them more. Or maybe not because sometimes I feel like I'm the black sheep in God's family. What I mean is it appears that everyone around me gets what they want, and I get what's left. Here lies the problem with me. I should only do the best I could do and not worry about them. Only believe I am living God's teachings and pleasing God. If I need a friend, I know God is available.

I do not wish to be your friend, nor do I wish to be your enemy.
It works for all that is pure of heart.
Now is better than *never*.

Bona Fide

Are we bona fide, or are we without direction? Do we mimic what others say and do? Do we have any sincerity? Do we copy others in the way they walk, the way they talk, and copy their gestures? Then the answer is no; we are not bona fide. Jesus is the most bona-fide person in this world. His sincerity is above reproach, and you will never find a more honest person than Jesus. Are you starting to get an understanding of what *bona fide* is? So many questions and not enough answers. Are we sincere to others? It's easier to copy others than have a genuine thought of your own. We try to be ourselves. First, we have to know what *bona fide* means. It means you have to be genuine, an individual among many. An individual who can create on their own. Create honest thoughts, create honest feelings, and all the while you are a genuine individual. There are so few leaders of an honest nature. There are many fakes and very dishonest people. We should try to reach out to them and help them mend their ways. It won't be easy, and yes, it is worth your time to make them godly, as Jesus would want you to. If you're the type who does nothing for anyone without being compensated, then forget that thought because you will be rewarded by our God; it may be monetary, or it may be peace within you, which is more valuable than gold. We should always work on ourselves to be a bona-fide individual. Start today. Don't waste another day. If you use a Tate's compass for direction, you will be lost because he who *hesitates* is lost.

God bless America and all its people who trust in God.

Bullying

To all people who went through this experience, be brave; the bully doesn't know you. It seems to give them a false ego. They are the ones who are lost in life's journey, not you. They thrive on making others miserable just to get them through the day, or sometimes, days. When you feel you are being disrespected at some point and they are talking to you, simply say, "No need to apologize. I forgive you." And walk away. In order for you to get through this, you must first believe in yourself. Build up your self-esteem and confidence. You know your life; they don't. If they see it's bothering you, they will do it that much more because this is what they thrive on. Oh, this also gives you an insight into the bully's life—so sad for them. They are the one who needs to be pitied. But that's God's department, not yours nor mine. They have to answer to him for their shortcomings. We should pray for them to see the errors of their ways. I always say when someone does something to you, whether it be verbal or physical, the first time, it hurts them; after that, the hurt is on you for going through the ordeal over and over in your mind. Forget it and move on. Life has a way of balancing out the good and the bad.

Let your inner beauty work its way out.
Even bad things come to an end.

Can You See Me?

Ｗe seem to always be in a hurry. Rush, rush, rush. I would like to just relax and see the world around me. It seems when I'm in line at a department store, the workers just go about their business as if I'm not there, like I am invisible. And then someone else walks to the counter alongside me, and the workers go to them immediately, as if I was not there. So frustrating. Then they finish helping the person who went ahead of me. At this point, I am beginning to get upset. Knowing I should remain calm. Suddenly, they wait for someone on the other side of the counter. Now I have to at least let them know I am waiting. So I make my presence aware, and they reply, "Please wait your turn." The people who went ahead of me should have acknowledged me, but they didn't. Being the polite person I am, I just made myself invisible by leaving—with my pride intact and thanking God for the wisdom.

Why is there more rain in some lives than others?
It works for all that is pure of heart.
Now is better than never.

Children's Thoughts

Dear Mom and Dad, I just turned twenty-one today. I'm not sure what that means, or why twenty-one seems to be a legal age for you to be free from the past. I guess now I am an adult. I don't seem to feel any different because of my age, maybe a little sad, or is that a little happy, I don't know. Life seemed to be easier when I was younger. When I didn't know something, I would simply go to Mom or Dad. Now it seems I should know what to do. I did when I was younger, or at least I thought so. So I wonder what changed. It seems one day should not have made that much difference. I wish all this responsibility was easier. Oh, when I was younger, I seemed to take things in stride. Maybe I did because you both were there for me. I am not forgetting Gram and Papa because they helped me to be a leader, not a follower. I sure do miss them. They were always there for me, and when I needed something, I just asked them. I don't ever remember them telling me no. They only said, "Be careful" and "We love you," as did you, Mom and Dad. There are so many things going through my mind right now. I'm not sure where to start. If only God could meet me halfway, I know I can finish my life on my own. I now know what to do because I just remembered what Papa used to say if he was talking to me or my sister, and we were troubled. He would say to me, "Man up," or to my sister, "Woman up." So with Jesus's help, I will just do that.

Excluding age, when does a child become an adult?

Circle Completed

This is the journey your soul will take after death. In this circle, we have four circles, one inside the other.

Note: See page of circles.

Circle 1 is the Earth (God's paradise): 100 percent.

Circle 2, we have heaven of which 80 percent of the souls go to.

Circle 3 is purgatory, of which 10 percent of the souls go. Purgatory is a holding station for souls that have not met God's expectations and must repent to move on to heaven. Only 2 percent of the souls here will repent, and 8 percent of the souls will remain in purgatory. When God sees there are so many souls in purgatory that is going nowhere (keep in mind, these 8 percent will not go to hell), eventually, God will destroy them as a group, and their souls will be no more. This creates new souls for God to send to Earth. These new souls have no past life.

The fourth circle is hell, of which 10 percent of the souls are sent. What I meant by *sent* is their souls go to heaven to be judged only to find out God is sending them to hell. Keep in mind, hell is not the end of this particular soul as Satan sends them to Earth to do his bidding. However, while on Earth, this soul sees its way is bad, and they repent (be born again on Earth) when they pass away (die); their soul again will be in front of God to be judged, and this time, God may accept this soul.

This circle will be completed many times over until God decides to destroy his paradise, and he will never do this as long as the Christians outnumber the nonbelievers by a great margin—80 percent or more.

God knows my life as well as he knows all his children's lives.

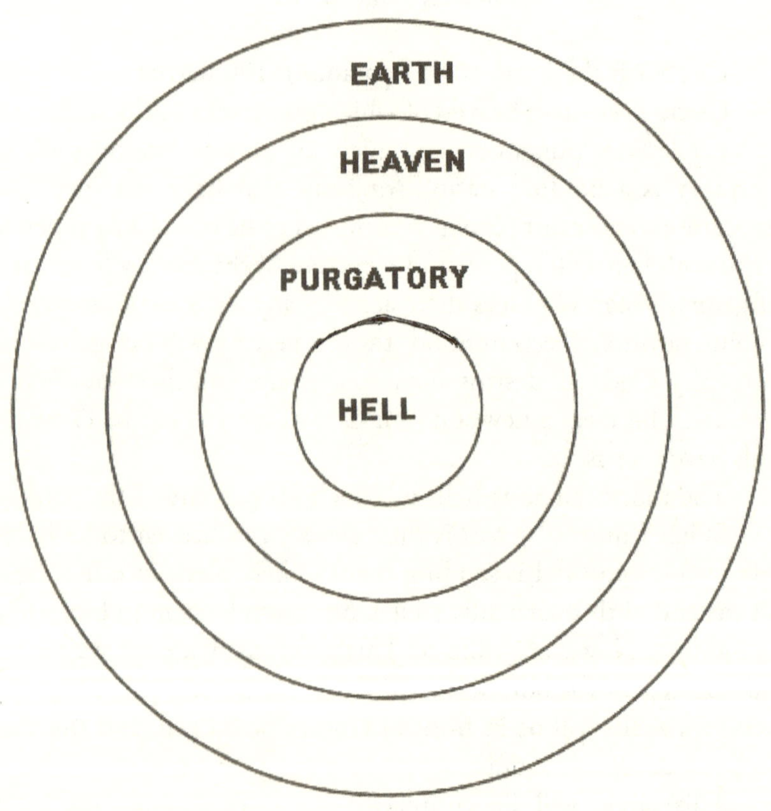

EARTH
HEAVEN
PURGATORY
HELL

Communion

Everyone, I suppose, has heard of communion. I don't think a lot of Christians know the meaning. Except the bread is Jesus's body, and the wine is his blood, which he gave his life so that you may believe and follow him spiritually. Jesus was crucified twice. I didn't know that. (*Did you?*) Once on the cross and once through Alan de la Roche. Jesus had the apostles gather around him and told then, "This is my body," and Jesus gave each a piece of bread. The he said to them with the wine, "Drink this. It is my blood, which I shed for all." He didn't just have one apostle at a time; he purposely shared this with them as a group. That is another reason to go to church (when you can) so that you can be with everyone at that mass to take communion (as a group). That is what Jesus meant—unity with one God, one paradise, one soul; and you are a great part of all his love for what God his father created. He wants you to love and understand yourself so you may pass that love for him to others. Don't let him be crucified in vain. Understand why his father had to take this drastic measure. Sometimes we are not aware of a situation until it hits home. And I believe that is what God tried to do: Make us aware of why Jesus died. When people have communion, they think it is just for them at mass. It is for them because you are pure at this time as you confess your sins. But it is for everyone who takes communion as a group. God loves all who come together to praise him.

Don't be afraid of life; embrace it.

Comparison

Everyone is different for the biggest part. We are different from one another; even twins or triplets are not the same. We only have the life that we are living now. We cannot remember our previous lives, so we cannot compare our future to the past. As we should not try to remember the past, always move forward. God knows our past, and he also knows our future. Because he made us. He does not want us to try to be like others; he wants all his creations to be themselves. The one thing he does want is for all of us to trust and believe in him. We are all special to our God. He does not choose one over the other, and most of all, he does not compare us to each other. You are you, and they are them. I believe God wants us to compare our life to his. To follow the right path. Also, try to remember all the saints, and I believe if you do, you will discover the one you are like and then make the comparison.

Always be glad that you are you.
It works for all that is pure of heart.
Now is better than *never.*

Compelling

I seem to have somewhat of a problem concentrating on most every-thing. I know my mind is alert, and my hearing is fine, so what's the problem? I try to pay attention when someone is talking to me. I also do the same when I am reading. The problem is when I am being spoken to, my mind seems to drift off slightly. Same with reading. Oh, I hear the words, and I see the words, but they seem to go in one ear and out the other. This happens when the subject they are on and telling me about it I really don't seem to care. I care about who is talking to me; it's the subject they're on that eludes me. So I listen to them go on and on, so I listen so as not to disrespect them. I am compelled to listen. I believe I need God to make me compelling. God needs to sit me down and say, "Relax, take your time, as I am not forcing you to do this. You must concentrate on things around you and remember what you saw and what you heard on your own." Your mind can be controlled by you, and if you let it, someone else may take over your mind and its thoughts. Are you paying attention right now? I didn't think so. I can see in your expressions that you are listening, and the letter you are reading you are not concentrating on. You seem to be somewhere else. I don't seem to be holding your attention. Do I have to shout or do cartwheels or make funny faces for you to pay attention to? I bet you will remember *that*. And I bet when you tell someone about *that*, you will know every detail. Just pay attention to God and his son Jesus. They will guide you through life.

I know two things and I just told you one.
Pay attention when I'm talking to you.

Conception

Having a child is a turning point in life for the mother, as it should be for the father. Whether the person in your body was planned or not is immaterial. That person in your body is a human being and a gift from God. Whether you realize it or not, that baby is yours to keep; love that child, and you will see the love that child will bring to you. Under certain circumstances, you may not be able to carry that child to birth. So sad, but as some of you know, it happens. Don't blame yourself or God. You are the guardian of that child and if you purposely ended a *healthy* child's life. Say a lot of Hail Marys because you will regret that decision for the rest of your life. Common sense should prevail—*something not very many people use in this age*. This is meant for some that had an abortion, under certain *conditions* or *circumstances*. Again, only God knows you. You have to live with that. God does forgive those who went through that, but only once in a lifetime. And we do have a forgiving God. Praying is good, and God is listening. Don't give up on yourself or God; you are still a good person, but mostly, remember the baby in your womb was once you. Of course, in your mother's womb. You may not be here if your mother took that drastic measure (abortion). Any man who has fathered a child should realize what the mother is going through, whether it be physical or mental. I want to thank all of you, Moms. You most certainly deserve it.

There is no answer to why.
Somebody does know your thoughts.

Confession

Confession is something that is necessary for all of us. We cannot carry the burden of sinning our whole life. So let's confess our sins. Your first thought must be, "Must I go to church to confess?" A good way of thinking, *but* (I really dislike the word *but*) sorry, back to what we were discussing. Confessions can be done in many ways, one of which is to tell a friend your sins, but I don't think we should go there. And the second way to confess is to yourself. Does that make any sense because I already know my sins? Believe me, so does God. Here is the difference. Start with a sin that you think is not a sin, but you are not sure it is. Well, it is, if you questioned it. After you say to God your sin, say a Hail Mary. The greater the sin in your mind, you may want to say many Hail Marys, also while saying them, try to see Mary's face. If you cannot, don't despair; you will. And please after each sin that you confess, always tell Jesus you love him. If you can, while doing the above, try to set at least fifteen minutes on a Sunday to do the confession. Now, let's go to church; that is a good idea. All the proper tools of confession are right at your fingertips. When you go to confession, try to do it responsibly. Don't keep repeating that same sin over and over; remain calm. Also don't hold back if you are ashamed of that sin as I'm sure the Father heard most everything. He will tell you your penance. Thank Father. *Note*: Believe you have been forgiven and move on.

Instead of putting up with Satan, evict him from your mind.
It works for all that is pure of heart.
Now is better than never.

Confounded

Today, I'm going to try to stay calm no matter who tries to annoy me. That's kinda funny because there is probably no way I can have a peaceful day. Someone is bound and determined to seek me out and irritate the heck out of me. I know they do it on purpose just to rile me. They wake up and say, "Let's annoy him today." At least, that's how I feel it happens. I think also it may seem that way because I look for it. And dwell on when someone annoys me. Every time I get to a happy place, someone invades my space. I love to be with most people, and for the most part, everything seems okay. And then someone ruins the moment with a comment that hurts me. I also know they never meant that the way I took it, but nonetheless, I felt the hurt. Of course, being the gentleman that I am, I let it slide without commenting. I feel that I am the better person for doing so, even if I felt like giving them the speech of their lives. Thank you, Jesus, for sparing me the embarrassment I would have gone through had you let me open my mouth. You are my inspiration, and I try to always do what you ask and try not to annoy and/or irritate anyone. Confound it.

Sometimes fantasy is better than reality.
Too many thoughts are wasted on a friendship.
Skip the sarcasm and just pretend to be friends.
It works for all that is pure of heart.
Now is better than never.

Conscience

What do you think? Your head houses your brain, and your brain houses your conscience. You probably are wondering where I'm going with this. Let me explain: When you think bad thoughts, you blame Satan; when you think good thoughts, you *forget* to thank Jesus. Sometimes we have to just take the blame; put the blame on ourselves. Leave Satan and God out of this. You don't need to be swayed by anyone. If you really think it's not you, go ahead and blame your thoughts. When a thought comes to mind, whether it be good or bad, your conscience tells you what direction to take. It all starts with how you think and how much you believe in our God. *Let me back up. Early on, I said leave God out of this. Well, we can't because God is always in our life whether we like it or not (so is Satan).* There are always two paths to take. One path is rough and muddy, and the other path is paved. Your conscience will tell you what path to take. Satan's job is to make you think the rough road is the right path; he really doesn't care which path you take, but we all have a job to do whether it be physical or mental. Be polite and tell Satan I know your way is the easiest, but thank you, anyway. I will take the path God chose for me. God's way always makes me feel vibrant and full of energy. His (God's) way makes me smile and makes me feel good about myself. Thank you, Jesus, and tell your father (God) we are with him in our thoughts, in our mind, and in our conscience; and we will always try to take the right path. Thank you for guiding me in the path of life. Love you.

God is in control of you, and you are in control of Satan.

Contribution

Most of the time, we feel so overwhelmed with life and the things in this world. I long for my childhood when we had very little. Someone who was fortunate to have more than one pair of shoes should realize how fortunate they were. Little things, you say! Walk in my single pair of shoes I had when I was growing up. Oh, by the way, the pair I had was split in the back; as a result, I could not run without my shoe falling off. So what you say! Well, because of that, I was not able to play sports in school, not because of my shoes falling off, but because I thought in my mind I couldn't run. So sad. Even with all said above, my contribution in this life was to help others with God's help. My contribution was to smile, be friendly, make others feel important, and love all people, so I feel that I contributed to this life. Thank you, Jesus, for contributing to make my life precious.

Sometimes I try to remember to forget.
It works for all that is pure of hear.
Now is better than never.

Controlled

Let's think about this word. This word is like the directions on a compass. It may lead you down a path you would never go. Someone may be controlling you. So sad, as that should never be. It may be when you are at a very young age and really don't know you're being controlled. Again, so sad. When we reach a certain age, we realize we have been manipulated into something we would never have done. So many paths and so many avenues. We trusted our parents to teach us about where to go and what to do. Sometimes, that is not the case. Again, so sad. We may have seen one of our parents take complete control of the other, and we did not know why, but we accepted it because we either were being controlled by the same person, or we simply did not know right from wrong. So sad to find out at a later date and time what was really going on. Try not to blame the one that's being controlled whether it be the mother, the father, or an aunt or uncle or another sibling. The fault lies with the perpetrator. They have to answer to God, and I believe he would give them a taste of their own medicine, as the saying goes. Back to you, now that you are an adult and have only bad memories of your childhood. The main thing is that it was *never* your fault. You just happened to be there. So sad. Please don't do the same to your child as what was done to you. Listen to God. I know when I'm troubled, God is always there for me. He will be there for you too. I'm sure God will cradle you in his arms and tell you it's all okay now; the worst is over, so enjoy what you have and who you have.

Don't be afraid of life.
Never look back only look ahead.
Always be glad that you are you.

Conundrum or Canard

Let's start with *conundrum*.

In God's world, it sometimes gets very confusing, especially when you wish for something and that something does not come to past. That's when we become puzzled as we thought when we are good, we should be rewarded and get what we want; that's what is so puzzling. It simply does not work that way, or we would be overwhelmed if we were to get all that we wished for. Not to mention unhappy or wanting even more. God will grant your wishes to match your lifestyle. If you want a better lifestyle, don't wish for it; work for it. Manual labor is always satisfying because you made it happen. Now the *canard*; life seems to play jokes on us. We think we know what's going on, only to find out we were misled, not by God but by our fellow humans. I know personally it bothers me to find out what I thought was real turned out to be a hoax. In closing with God's help, I will overcome all canards, and I know God will help me solve my mysteries.

You must feel good enough about yourself to believe prayer works.
It works for all that is pure of heart.
Now is better than never.

Creation of Races

God made Adam and then created Eve from Adam. Adam's body was made from dust. Eve's body was made from Adam's body. Because Eve's body came from man, this is where genetics came from. The different genes in the human body (same with animals). Keep in mind at this point in time there was only one huge world, which he (God) called his and yours, paradise. Only love and beauty. And only populated by Adam and Eve. God needed his paradise to be populated with more people. *(Please understand what I'm about to say is not personal, only common sense. Please forgive me if I am offending you, which is not my intention.)* So this is where it all started with Adam and Eve's offsprings. I think eighteen girls and twenty-two boys. Their children had children, and their children had children. How can this be? It all has to do with interbreeding.

Remember at this point in time, it was God's intention to populate the Earth. As time went on, God intended that to change, only cousins should have offsprings. But only to a certain point in time, which God set. If this course of action were kept within God's timeline, all would have been okay. But that was not the case because some of God's children only thought of themselves, not God's word. So the wrong crossbreeding continued for thousands of years. This made God very angry. Even God thinks enough is enough, and this disrespect of him (God) changed the world. At this point in time, God had Noah build an ark. God did not tell Noah why, and Noah respected God's wishes and built the ark to God's specifications. It was to be able to hold all two of God's creatures—one male and one female—as well as Noah and his wife and their three children and their wives. After the ark was built and all was aboard, God made it rain forty days and nights to destroy all that was not on the ark. After the water subsided, it was now Noah's job to repopulate the Earth. Most of this population had to come from his three sons: Shem and Ham and Japeth.

The three sons went in different directions. (Reminder, they did not want to go in different directions as God intended, so he took steps to make this happen, as explained in the creations of life.) I believe Shem went to what we now call the east, and Ham went to a warmer climate, which is what we now call Africa. And Japeth kind of stayed around home, I think.

Keep in mind, at this point in time, there was still one world (God's paradise). When the brothers reached their destination, they began to populate the area they were in. Being human and the population getting bigger (same as the beginning, so I won't mention crossbreeding), men, not God, divided up his world. Shem's side of the world was the East, also known as the orient. And for Ham, it was Africa, as it is called now by history. This is now the setting for all races on Earth. This setting took place in the years from Adam to Noah. The different genes were in the three sons before the ark and mixed genes can and do have an effect on all things that make up different races. It can make the bodies look different from one another as the orient have their color and body shape, and people in Africa have their color and shape. Ham's skin was darker in color, and Shem's skin was lighter—all from different breeding.

Now that the population was getting bigger, and the world was filled with different races, all races have a leader at this point in time. Some leaders are greedy, or maybe they just needed more space, so this is how wars began (another subject), and just like before (Adam and Noah's time), the only thing changed was man created territories and nations. And the world was divided in more ways than one. All was supposed to be to thank God and do his bidding. Not working out again because of non-Christians—people who do not believe in God, so sad. One day, when their soul is face-to-face with God, it would be too late at this point in time. Now history always seems to repeat itself. So now, it went from Adam to Noah, and now is on its way to Moses and the Ten Commandments. In my opinion, this was how different races and nations began. At an earlier point in time, probably after Noah, God changed the living part of life. Instead of living a short life, as an example, others can reach nine hundred or more years. God decides to limit man's age. I guess maybe God figured man could do less damage to his world if he lived fewer years. In my opinion, I am not a cynical person. All I know is I am here in God's paradise to serve God in this life and all other lives he permits me. I hope you can do the same.

Cremation

This is a private letter between me and my God. We lived all our life. No matter how many years our soul spent in this body. This is the body God gave me to house my soul. It belongs to him (God). Our body is a work of art, whether it be a woman or a man. God created you and me. Some are happy with their body, and some are not. Why is that? We see some who seem to be perfect in our eyes. That is a mistake because God made us all the same; you have to look inside to see the true beauty; God made us all equal on the inside. Sometimes we try to alter what God has given us. Sometimes it is necessary to make changes on the outside, whatever makes you happy. We should be happy and faithful to what God gave us to work with. We sometimes are a little overweight, and sometimes, we are too thin. If you are healthy and happy in that state, so be it. It is your body from God, and it is just a loaned piece, so take care of it as if it is your most valuable possession. We are in charge of us on Earth. We make our own decisions. God will help us with those decisions as long as we are faithful to him (God). Stay happy; stay healthy. You will one day meet our God face-to-face. Not your body but your soul. Don't be afraid; all is well. While your soul makes its journey to heaven, your body is an empty shell. And one way or another, it will turn to dust. Also God wants your remains returned to the paradise he made (Earth) whether it be by burial or cremation—that is your decision as long as it is returned to Earth. Again, do not dwell on this nor be afraid. You will be in good hands.

Remember, death is not the end, just a new beginning.

Deception

Who are we, and why are we here? We all are children of God. We also try to do our best from the time we are able to think for ourselves. Sometimes our thinking is not our views but someone else's views, and we are being influenced by others and being deceived. It could come from family, friends, or even our traditions. We sometimes fall into a pattern and believe that's the way it is and always will be that way. Follow your heart; God will lead you. You will not be deceived by our God—*yes, our God.* If you were raised by parents or anyone who does not believe there is a God, you are being deceived into thinking you are just here and have no idea why. I will try to tell you why (my views). You are being given the opportunity to start your life at any age if you follow your heart. You are not being disrespectful or defiant. You are realizing you are you and not them (the unbelievers). Pray for them to follow you, and in time, the unbelievers will believe. Thanks to you.

Why are you afraid to ask for help?
It works for all that is pure of heart.
Now is better than *never.*

Denouncing

Anytime you feel you've been let down, you feel betrayed. It can be by a best friend or by someone you just happen to know. Sometimes when we believe so strongly in someone, it hurts even worse. Someone you worshipped all your life and tried to do the right thing, and you feel betrayed. Sometimes the pressures of life can get you down—really, really, really, down. So we need to blame someone besides ourselves. So we denounce them. Life gets a bit scary when and if you have ever reached that point. Some of us have, and we were not strong enough at the time to weather our storm, so we blame God, when in reality, we should remember the good things in life and how God led us through troubled waters. God made us strong, and we lost some or most of our strength from these trying times. If you have ever denounced God, don't feel like you can never be forgiven because God will forgive you as he has forgiven me (three times), and I guarantee you, there will never be a fourth for me. My love for my God is deeper than life itself. Thank you for my life, Jesus.

Let me help carry that burden.
It works for all that is pure of heart.
Now is better than never.

Despair

You wake up to another day of sorrow. Why is that? The days do not change; the weather may. We don't like to see a lot of rain. We love the sunshine because it relates to smiling, and rain relates to frowns. We all have our own personal rain cloud—sometimes not by choice, or maybe it is without us realizing it. It may be that your friends only tell you about the bad news, and then you proceed to tell them our story of even worse news, thinking even worse news makes them feel better. Sometimes we should stop after hearing their bad news, forget our bad news, and tell them something that will cheer them up. It may also cheer you up, as good news seems to do just that. We don't have to give in to despair because of seemingly hopeless situations. If we dwell on the things that make us feel hopeless, days and nights will pass, and we will feel there is no hope. There is hope for all of us in God. Please wait; hear me out before you shake your head. God made you, and he will protect you. Shake the devil (our despairing thoughts), and you will start to feel the freedom from despair. Love yourselves and God. In God, we trust to rid us of all hopelessness. You deserve to be happy. Thank you, Jesus.

Happiness is contagious and so is sorrow.
(Jerry Manukin)

Divergent

We all have our divergencies. Most of the time, we do not agree on a variety of subjects. We try to convince anyone who will listen to us to agree on what we are talking about, but a lot of the time, the other party or parties go in a different direction. One subject that is very divergent is religion; even though we have different opinions, we are still talking about one God for all. More often than not, our divergence takes us on a different path or course. We should listen to others and not rush to judgment on the subject they are talking about because, who knows, they may be right. Even if we do not agree at the time, later we may realize they knew what they were talking about. But human nature such as it is, we still may not acknowledge what we learned from them. We may even take a different path than we were on because of our new knowledge on that particular subject. Some may even make others believe they came up on this as their own. But we will never do that. When we were born God made us think and love the same. Somewhere along the way, we started to get different opinions. On a lot of things. But that's okay because those paths are subject to change. Your destiny will not change, so let us keep an open mind.

You must follow God and lead others.
Skip the sarcasm, and just pretend to be friends.

Don't Be Afraid to Cry

Sometimes I get myself all worked up over things—sometimes things that shouldn't bother me, but they do anyway. I suppose that's on me, which makes it worse. It would be better and more understandable if it were you making me feel this way. But, alas, it's on me. So sad. I feel like just letting it all out and having a good cry, but I am an adult now, and adults aren't supposed to cry. I don't know who started that saying; after all, it is just a saying. Maybe no one started it—it is probably just a part of life. Again, so sad. I awoke this morning thinking, "I hope I can just be me today." Me, like I was when I was ten. If something bothered me or something hurt me, I wasn't afraid to cry. It sure did make me feel good after my cry. Probably it felt so good because my mom or dad would cradle me in their arms and tell me, "Everything's okay now." Now I know things are going to be different in my mind from now on because I know if my husband knew how I felt, he would tell me to just let it all out. He would cradle me in his arms and give me comfort in my troubled times.

Smiles and laughter are not only what others do
(Jerry Manukin, 07-28-2024)

Exalt

When I think of my wife and son and daughter, I am thankful for them, and I couldn't begin to think how my life would be without them. They all blossomed into Christians and loving all and each other as a family unit. They all try to understand everyone's feelings and would do no harm to any one intentionally. They all know the way the world works from God's perspective. They take care of their children and taught them to be Christians. We are a holy family by honoring God and his son Jesus and each other and most of you. That last thought was for me only because they honor and respect all that comes in contact with them. Me, not so much. But I am trying. We all learn from each other about God and life. That exalts us higher in God's eyes to take another few steps up his mountain. We may never reach the top of his mountain, but in this life, we take another step higher every day. And that not only pleases our God; it also pleases me. Thank you, Jesus, for making this possible. *My family.*

This day will end with or without me.
Sometimes the things I think about are not my thoughts.
Jesus is not only a way out, but a way in.
Time is on your side, mine is limited.

Faithful

Faithful is a word that is very complicated. Let us try to work on this one together. So many places to start and only one place to end. Let's go from the bottom up in this case. The bottom line is, should we be faithful to people who only try to make us unhappy and sad all the time? Let's not confuse faithfulness with loyalty. Sometimes we have to put ourselves on top of the list; no, it's not selfishness. It's keeping our sanity, which is sometimes overrated (sanity, I mean, is overrated). Moving on, let us think about being faithful to Jesus; after all, he has done so much for us and is still doing for us. So let's think about being faithful to Jesus. As we know, bad news is usually very depressing and sometimes uncontrollable. Jesus is about good news, which we all like to hear. And I would like to feel that God is so proud of us as he created us. God is perfect as is his son Jesus. We also are his children, so let us be faithful to both and make them proud.

You can live your normal life and still love God.
It works for all that is pure of heart.
Now is better than never.

Family Tree

I am just a branch on my family tree. This tree is for my relatives and their families. If I were to go back in time, my family tree would be a forest. So let's not complicate things and talk about the family members on my family tree in this life (my life). How many times have we heard someone say about a loved one, whether it be a wife or husband or mother and father or a sister or brother or just a loved one, "I will be with them in heaven" (*not taking away from your beliefs*). But your loved ones are and should be only a memory. Because I believe they (their soul) are about to continue their life on another family tree. Don't be sad; it is a good thing the way God sets up family trees. If you want to help a deceased relative on your family tree, pray to God and ask him to send a guardian angel from heaven to whomever you want (*you should say their names*) for them to have a blessing in their new life. Love and life are an eternity. Life has a beginning but has no end even after death. As an example, if you lost a loved one three years ago, that person (soul) is now three years old in their new life.

Feelings

How do you feel? What I'm asking is not if you feel okay or if you are well. No, I'm asking how you feel inside. Are you bothered by something that was said to you or something you heard? Did you interpret what you thought they said? Did that hurt your feelings? Remember, they are not doing this to you—you are doing this to yourself because of your feelings. Also, remember that not all feelings are bad or hurtful. Your heart sends your feelings to your brain, and you take over from there. You can continue to dwell on your hurt feelings, or you can dwell on your happy feelings. Controlling your feelings is the key to good feelings. If you don't let go of the hurt feelings, you will carry a sad face. It seems when we are hurt, we do not let go as easily as we let go of our good feelings. Love in your heart is good for you, and it also improves your health. Don't blame God for your feelings—this one is on you and you alone. Sometimes we should just say, "You hurt my feelings." Confession is good for you, as we all know. But be careful who you confess to. Also, you can be hurt by what was not said to you. Feelings are complicated. So to sum up, don't dwell on your feelings, good or bad. Just be happy; don't let your heart feel so heavy. Love will put your heart on a diet.

Follow

The world is filled with followers. When we are with a group, we follow them. That's okay if you are on a guided tour; however, if not, you should think long and hard about who you should follow. God will judge you on you, not the group you follow. He is fixed on you as an individual. Make your decisions wisely as it *is* a matter of life and death. If your conscience tells you don't go there, then don't go there; it really is that simple. Your life will be filled with love and happiness as long as you follow *him*. Are you wondering why I did not say follow Jesus? The reason I didn't was I wanted to see if you knew *him*; now think back to when I said *him*. What was your first thought? That will tell, you if you didn't know it was Jesus, then who? Always follow Jesus and keep him (Jesus) in your thoughts. If you want people to follow you, then lead them into prayers.

If you want to follow, follow your dreams.
It works for all that is pure of heart.
Now is better than never.

Footprints

When I take a stroll down by the waters in the sand, I can say that I never leave any footprints. Or maybe that's what I would like to think. As God has told me never to look back so I don't know if there are footprints. Life is like that; we don't leave footprints. We would like to. So why don't we? We all should strive to give blessings to our fellow man. We should only say kind things about everyone even if we keep the opposite to ourselves. Those are the footprints God and his son Jesus would like all of us to leave. That is their goal for all their children. Since I brought up children, it is Christmastime again; we must never forget what Christmas is. We think of presents for all; don't forget where you got the money for those gifts for your family and others. The money is a gift to you from God and his son Jesus. Don't forget that. Now about Christmas. It is Jesus's birthday; he gave you the means to survive in this world. So where is his gift? He doesn't want material things like us. He only asks for your love for him and his world. So little to give for a life he has given us. I personally cannot survive my days and nights without him. I will strive to make him (Jesus) proud of me. And to tell him and my family I will try to leave footprints ahead of me instead of behind me and that they all have my love.

Merry Christmas.

Freedom

J ust think about the word *freedom* and what it actually stands for and what it should mean to you. A lot of people do not realize how free America is, and some abuse that freedom. Mostly, some don't realize the freedom they have because they have nothing to compare it too. A little research will help you understand; look up other countries and nations, and compare their freedom to ours. You then will realize what you have living in the United States of America and the American flag, which is so beautiful should be cherished, not desecrated. You should get chills and maybe a little tearful when our national anthem is being played. Freedom has its limits; please don't exceed what God gave you in his country, and please do not hate your country. It may be you hate someone or you hate certain rules; however, those rules are the same for everyone. Don't feel like you are better than anyone because they may feel that way about you. You will find out what freedom means when you take that chip off your shoulder. Let us all work together for our God and our country. You are being singled out only in your mind. God treats everyone the same, but only if you have God in your life. That is, freedom. If not removed, the chip you have on your shoulder may become a log.

Some people are free, and they still feel unfree.
It works for all that is pure of heart.
Now is better than never.

God Knows

I always look forward to celebrating easter. God made me human, and he protects me and all humanity, which is why he gave his life for all of us. This is why I look forward to easter to remind me of Jesus suffering. Compared to what he went through for us, I have no pain. Let me take the time to remind you of how he felt in his last hours of living. To show his love, he said to his father, "Forgive them, for they no not what they do." He was not just talking about the ones who crucified him; he was talking about you and me. Also, one of his final words was to John, saying, "Take care of my mother." He meant that not only for his mother; he meant for all of us to take care of our mothers. The things that must have gone through Jesus's mind we will never know. He asked his father in heaven, "Why did you forsake me?" That was a rhetorical question to God because he (Jesus) already knew the answer. The people around the cross were speaking badly of him, including the person on his left on another cross. The one being crucified on the right felt Jesus's pain and said to him how he felt and that Jesus did not merit being crucified, and they (the two men on both sides of Jesus) deserved to be punished. Jesus forgave the man who repented and said to him, "You will be with me in paradise." Jesus said to the crucifiers, "I thirst." The crucifiers gave him vinegar to drink. Jesus, at this time, said, "My work is done. It is finished as I did what my father commanded me to do, and I faithfully carried out his wishes. Now that I have fulfilled my duties, I can commend my spirit to you (God)," and he then reunited with his father in heaven. His duties were now paid in full.

Easter Sunday 2024

God, Satan, You

God tries to make us Christians. Satan tries to make us do what is against Christianity. Most who preach reference the Bible and form their opinion of what was read. Their version may differ from yours and your interpretation of the same passage. I have read the Bible, and what confuses me is that they are all right. How can that be? They cannot all be right. When I look at a passage in the Bible, I consider every angle of that one passage, as it is not always self-explanatory. I read between the lines so I know exactly what was said. And now I have the whole truth of God.

Let's move on to Satan's role. God is always right, and Satan tries to turn God's rights into wrongs. Satan doesn't care what you believe—he is there to make your life a living hell. So what are we going to do about him? I have the answer to that and more. What I do is pray for Satan. Why, you ask? Here's an example: One of your so-called friends likes to get on your nerves. If you argue back, this could go on indefinitely. We don't want that, so we try to be nice to them, and they can't understand you being nice. They want it to be like it was—hectic. Now you've confused them, and it worked. So why not confuse Satan as you did your friend? Even though Satan is not your friend, let's pray for Satan, and with that said, he will move on because Satan likes to be the boss of you.

Now here's the punch line: When you pray for yourself or someone else, say your prayer to God, and after that, ask Satan not to interfere in your life or theirs, and he will oblige. Also, when something happens to you, whether you knock something off the table or it rains on your parade, remember it is your fault, not Satan's. Things happen. You now have the upper hand—God gave you the strength to be strong. He doesn't care if you know Satan personally. He wants you to pray for your enemies, and that includes Satan. That's why we say, "God bless America."

Grace

We eat our snacks and meals without realizing we never thanked God for providing us with this food. It is no sin not to say grace, but we should be grateful we have this food to eat. When I was growing up from childhood to adulthood, some never thought to give thanks because there was a farm nearby, and they always went to the farm where great meals were provided. Moving forward, when I wed, I mentioned to my wife, "Tell me anything, such as we have no money for rent, or these bills becoming due, but please do not tell me we have no food to eat." Even a lard sandwich is food or a bologna sandwich or simply a slice of bread. In this day and age, we very rarely plant a garden, not because we do not want to, but because the interstate and cities took over the lands. That, I suppose, is progress; however, it is a good thing and a bad thing as it takes away farmlands and the forests where the animals live and feed. We all should get used to saying grace. Try it. You will feel the warmth that it brings (saying grace); in my mind, I like to say my grace in my way: Thank you, Father, for this food I am about to eat. And please, God, give the homeless and the hungry a slice of bread. In the name of the Father and the Son and the Holy Spirit (sign of the cross).

Pick your own way to thank God.
Jesus is not only a way out, but a way in.
It works for all that is pure of heart.
Now is better than never.

My Granddaughter

We would like you to know how proud we are of you. We think and pray every day that you are happy and have a beautiful day. If the days would match your beauty, life could be so beautiful. If it's possible for you, I would like you to go to church at least once a month with Gram. Getting started is the hard part. I know it is for me (Papa) as my days are full. The difference for me is that Jesus guides my life. He told me to send this to you spiritually. Most of the time, I listen to him, and this is one time I'm glad I did. I think with his help we can work out any problem that's bothering us. Oh, I know you had eighteen years of religion. But remember that was then, and this is now. With me, I can never get enough help to get me through some days. I'm not comparing my life to yours as only you know what's going on in your life and mind. This is why I am sending you a letter I call Tribulations. I know it fits me and helps my life and hoping it does the same for you. I shed many tears thinking about you. They are tears of *joy* just for you to be in our lives, especially being my granddaughter. Don't waste your life thinking.

PS: The letter I am referring to is in this book.
Love you with all our hearts.
Gram and Papa

With out you knowing this, you help me
get through some tough days.

Gratitude

So many ways to show gratitude for doing a good job or for just being kind. My favorite way to show gratitude is to not say thanks all the time but to simply smile. Remember, a smile is not a grin or a smirk; that's the opposite of thanks. People know how to read a smile, and they know what you mean because they interpreted your smile, which, in their eyes, shows disappointment, not gratitude. Now for saying the old standby, which is common, and sometimes, just a habit is thanks or thank-you. As you feel the person or persons did you a favor you appreciated, you might say thank-you so much. That thank-you is limited because it sets limits on how grateful you really are. I'm talking about the so-much part. Now someone helped you out by doing you a favor and to show your gratitude you say thank-you very much (a little better than so much); now someone helped you out of a more serious jam like making you a short-term loan and showing your gratitude for this, you may say thank-you very, very much. The more loan you take, you probably should add a couple more "verys," such as "Thank you very, very, very, very much." I'm sure you get the picture. Now the one you should thank by using a thousand or more verys is our God and his son Jesus. He shows you respect and gratitude many times over. Sometimes, when you feel like thanking God, just say "You're welcome" because he knows you were honest with him. Also, he doesn't expect thanks in any form; he just expects loyalty from you, which is your way of thanking him.

Thank you with all my love
(my way to show gratitude).

Gripes

Why do people constantly whine about the same thing over and over? Same person, different subject—very annoying. I hear the same thing about any subject over and over and over no matter who it is or where I'm at. It's so hard to be around someone who whines every time I see them and hear them. It has to be just as annoying to you and others as it is for me. Sometimes I feel like I should not even be in a public place as it is so annoying to hear this 24–7. I know it can't be as bad as it's made out to be, or maybe it is. I'm not sure. I try to remain silent and tell myself, *Be quiet.* Don't open your mouth as you should not form an opinion. After a period of time passing, it becomes a habit, and you never learn to just remain silent. After you leave and you are alone, you feel terrible and all you think about the day that you left and pray to God tomorrow will be different. I certainly hope so because hearing griping constantly is taking its toll on me to the point that I am very distressed. So I need to talk to God to give me the courage and strength I need to move forward in a different direction so as not to be frustrated all the time. I like happy endings, so if you didn't realize who I am talking about who is so annoying.

It's me. Yes, sometimes I can't stand to be around myself. I sure hope my actions can change to be silent thoughts for only me to hear. Have a nice day, if you want to.

I can't wait for tomorrow.

Happy Birthday

W ell, it's here again. When we were younger, we couldn't wait for our birthday to get here. Same for at least twenty-one years. Then we kinda shied away from birthdays. Not completely because birthdays are always fun, especially when they are shared with someone who loves you. You should be happy when you have a birthday. No matter what age you are. Oh, you don't feel that way. I can tell from the look on your face that you disagree. You disagree because you are getting older. Let me tell you why you should enjoy your birthday. Let's start with how God made you beautiful. It didn't just happen; God picked you personally. And he wanted you to share that beauty with all you know. Let's go another route. When your birthday comes around next year, what's your first thought? Mine would be, "Thank God I have another birthday, and please, God, let me continue to have birthdays for many more years to come. Your wife/husband loves to be with you and their thoughts are the same. I can't wait for another birthday. Hold it; I didn't mean for it to seem like a week I want it to feel like a long and happy year to spend with my loved ones. And especially, it gives me time to tell people about you (God and his Son Jesus). Thank you for the gift of love."

Now let me tell you how I feel personally.

When I look at you, I thank God you let me share your birthdays with me. I love you. Xoxoxoxo

 (Your wife/husband) 

Happy Days

When we look back into the past, sometimes we say, "That were the good old days." And as memories pass, they seem to be exaggerated into more than they actually were. I hope they were all happy. But somehow, I can't imagine that was the case. On the other hand, cling to those memories of the good old days. Sometimes things are always better in our minds and some worse. But we will forget those days and always remember the good days. Don't dismiss the thought of these days being terrible because they are not and no worse than the days of old. There are many times we have a good day. Our thoughts seem to always hang on the bad things. This is why the things I try to remember I forget, and the things I try to forget, I remember. One thing we never want to forget is that Jesus makes our days good and the other guy, let's not even mention his title as he has no part in our lives; we only have one room, and it is occupied by Jesus.

My goal is to make me happy.
It works for all that is pure of heart.
Now is better than never.

Heartache

Please don't confuse heart pain with heartache, as heart pain could be fatal, whereas heartache is a distraction. We see things around us that make our heart ache. Heartache is a feeling we have. It could be mild, or it could really make you lose a day through your mind as you only dwell on what made your heart ache. Some of the things I'm talking about is you may be watching television and seeing some things that you really do not like, so it makes your heart ache. Another thing may be your friends, who seem to always say something to you that upsets you. You hear and see all this, and ultimately, it ends up in your heart. I'm sure we all know about love; that may be the worst kind of heartache. The other things I mentioned can go away very quickly if you let it. Love, on the other hand, not so easy to let go. Mostly because it affects you directly. Your mind and your body can cause the heartache you feel. To handle this heartache (love), give it your best, and if that doesn't work, transfer what your heart feels to your brain. God will let you make the right decision. If it's separation from whom you received the heartache, so be it. Do not dwell on the separation as it will prolong your feeling better, and your heartache will linger on. After a little while, when you settle down, you will feel a different feeling in your heart. That is what's called happiness—a wonderful feeling, that you so rightly deserve. Thank you, Jesus, for the will power to help me make correct decisions. My heart doesn't ache anymore. And I smile a lot now. Also, I see the beauty everywhere I look.

I believe in God. Also, I believe in me.

Heaven's Journey A

I believe we all, at one time or another, think about what happens when we pass away (die). I know I have. I am not afraid because I lived my life the Christian way (almost always). But nonetheless, I do think about it. Rather than say death or dying, I will say we should never dwell on it. Nature will take its course when the time comes. Sometimes, it comes too soon for some and not fast enough for others. Let's start with too soon. Accidents happen. Now for the not-too-soon people, think positive, not negative. You are dwelling too much on it and not letting life take its course.

If the course you are on makes you feel that way. Start a new beginning in your mind, and this time, believe our God is on your side and wants you to feel beautiful or handsome, whatever the case may be. You can do it. If you don't believe in yourself, I do. And I know God does. Beauty is not always what you see but what you do and say. Now that that's out of the way, and for whatever reason, our journey begins, a deep sleep that releases your soul. That soul is now on its journey. When your soul reaches heaven's gate, your soul will now report to God. God will review what your soul has kept notes on. It will be in the form of a golden diary of only you, the good, the bad, and all in between.

Remember, your soul has no say or influence on this subject. It is between you and your creator to be judged on this lifetime you spent on Earth. God will go over the diary. PS: He already knows, but he wants to decide when and where to send your soul into the new life. Now is where the *judgment day* comes in. God will decide your fate. (You may be turned over to Satan, God forbid.) We will get to the journey to hell in the next letter. If you lived your life the Christian way, nothing more, he (God) will send your soul on your way to Earth to a new beginning and a new body. However, you will only be in this new life as happy or unhappy as you were in your old life, and your memory will be erased about the old life. Now let's move on to the ones who did more for their fellow humans than they had to. They will be given a new life with more happiness than they could imagine as a reward. Wait, there's more; if you lived your life for God and his children all your life, like loving his son Jesus and following most of God's Ten Commandments, you will be taken care of in your new life. And you will only improve in your happiness on Earth. You will receive many, many rewards and happiness. Again, you will not have any memory of the past, although somewhere along the way, you will think, "Hey, I remember this." Although in this life, you have never been there. Your soul will go on living and keeping notes of this life. Also, these notes are for this life now, not the past. For all of you who make it into heaven, you (your soul) will remain in heaven for a while, some longer than others, for God to reset your soul. Now you are back.

Do not waste your precious life in this round. Listen to your mind when it tells you things and then listen to your conscience. That's what life is about. And as I've said before, only God can end your soul and his paradise. We still have time. So let's believe in God and his son Jesus, and there will be a lot of todays and no yesterday and a lot of tomorrows.

You don't have to shout for God to hear you.
This is not what I do; this is what I did.
I bring good luck to bad people.
My life is a story yet to be told.
Life has no reverse.

Hell's Journey

When we went to heaven, our fate was decided by God. If God decides to turn you over to Satan at this time, your soul is headed in a completely different atmosphere. You are now a ward of Satan's. In Satan's world, you have no choices; you do just as you are told or suffer his (Satan's) wrath, which is severe. He has no pity on you, nor does he want to. You thought you were really something on Earth, a terrible person, and you enjoyed making others miserable. Guess what? It is now your turn; as the saying goes, what goes around comes around. Well, it's here. And there is nothing at this time you can do about it. Wait, there is something you can do. When Satan decides to send you back to Earth to do his bidding. Your conscience tries to tell you to straighten up, but you don't listen to your conscience. You didn't in your previous life, and if you don't in this life, learn to enjoy hell because you will stay there forever unless you use this lifetime to repent. When your soul returns to heaven, *remember, the reason your soul is back in front of our God, as he (God) owns your soul no matter where it goes.* God will review your soul's information, and this time, God may forgive you. So you see, God is a forgiving God, and he does not want you to suffer or do harm to others. Your fate is in your hands on Earth. (So repent.) After that, it's out of your hands.

Don't put off praying and giving thanks.

Help Me

I pray every day that what goes through my mind goes away. I need you, Jesus. I try to be myself as the person that's inside me is not me. The person inside me thrives on misery. I do not. I don't have a dual life; there's only me. I know my family loves me, and I know I love my family, so why do I do the things I do and act the way I do? Please help me. *I will help you* with the help of our God as I cannot do this alone. I can try, but your well-being means too much to me to give you bad advice. I know you probably heard what I am going to say a thousand times over from thousands of people. Or it seems so.

I asked God to help me to help *you and me* as I am in good standing with God the father and Jesus his son. They told me while I was sleeping what to say. So here goes. You need to find something to occupy your mind; you need to take back your mind, which is being controlled by someone or something without you realizing it. If you have a slight thinking problem, don't give in to your thoughts. God needs you to help him even though you feel you, or I cannot help ourselves. Let God occupy your mind, as he does mine. If it's a bipolar thing, you can and will be strong enough to overcome even that. God has the cure for all things. And he will cure you. Try to listen to yourself before the words leave your mouth. And compose yourself. Do I want someone to say that to me? If you don't like what you're about to say, don't say it. Simply, move on. Don't let your thinking make your life unbearable. Keep busy and help others. God said the break you are waiting for is now here. Thank you, Jesus. I will try my best, and I will never give up.

Here's Looking at You

If you're troubled, look in the mirror. When you see what you see, close your eyes and change that image to whomever or whatever is upsetting you. Now you are face-to-face with your problem. And try to understand the image's side; if things seem to be unclear of what you see, now it's your turn to speak. Say exactly what's on your mind—why you feel the way you feel, why you are troubled with them or it. You will not be interrupted, so take your time. After you have gotten what was bothering you off your chest and mind, take a deep breath now that it's almost over. At no point of the time you looked in the mirror, you should ever take your eyes away from the image. Why? Because you are feeling guilty, and this whole process is wasted. Now after you are satisfied you have said what needed to be said, open your eyes, and when you are face-to-face with your image, a smile will appear on your face. You will leave that smiling image on the mirror as you can now turn away, and you will be free. Love God and yourself. Those are the important people in your life.

Choose your friends wisely.

Hey, You

Hey, you, yes, I mean you. What's your problem? Why do you think you're the only one that matters? You're not alone; there are others just like you. Maybe you should start a club so that you will be around your kind. You seem to be the instigator of all problems between family and friends. So again, what's your problem? Could it be that when you were a child, someone was mean to you? Maybe it was a teacher who disliked you. Maybe it was a family member who took advantage of you. It could be a million things in your past, or it could be one isolated incident that you just can't let go. Stop and think. Why do you think people feel this way about you? And you feel about them. I'm sure somewhere along your path, you met someone you felt comfortable with, but that changed when you couldn't let go of your anger. Maybe anger is too harsh, so let's just say your past and *let it go at that*, as the saying goes. You chose to be a loner; not everyone else you are taking it out on *is out to get you*—again, as the saying goes. If this letter seems to fit your life, change your life, as only you can, with Jesus's help; and not only will you see the love, but you will also feel the love in this world. Disband your old club and join the human race.

If this letter offends you, it hits too close to
home and should be a wake-up call.

Hope

We must always cling to hope. Hope is not just another word; hope is life itself. With that said, we must always cherish life. At some point in life, we sometimes seem to have our backs on the wall. There seems to be nowhere to go, no way out of what's troubling us. Not so. Please, please stop and just for a moment take a deep breath. Breathing helps your body and mind. I almost always say, "Quit thinking." Well, in this case, I am not going to say that. I want you to think, and if necessary, think out loud. And also, while your back is to the wall, don't be afraid to scream—scream as loud as you can, maybe multiple screams. Then you will have heard your cries for help and realize you have broken the trance you were in at that wall. Welcome back to the world of the living. You now realize you can fix what's broken and move away from that wall. The only thing that has expired was that ride you were going to take on that long black train. It has left the station and will never come back. If you're not a religious person, that's okay—well, maybe not—but nonetheless, God heard your cries and screams, and he helped where others didn't seem to hear your cries. God is listening. Talk to him. Your secrets are safe with God. Then your life will be filled with amazing grace.

If you listen hard enough you can hear the silence.
(Jerry Manukin, 08-22-2024)

How Low Can We Get?

Life sometimes is not as you wish. You try very hard to do the right thing, and the more you try, it seems to get worse. Why is that? I'm not sure, but I believe the world calls it being in a rut. So how do we get out of that rut? Unfortunately, it is not that easy. You count on God to get us through these rough times, but for some unknown reason, he doesn't seem to come through for us. So as a result, we believe we must have done something wrong to offend him. *Do not go there; he is there.* So we must control our minds and believe we did nothing wrong, and even if we did, God forgave us through confession, so we must believe that. We need help now, so we must count on ourselves to get out of that rut. If we also know we are good people, and we try to believe in ourselves, we are stronger than we think. We must think positive thoughts to feel good and get our thoughts on the right track. We do believe in ourselves, and we are strong enough to overcome all circumstances and objects that are holding us back. The rut will come to an end, and when it does, thank God for the wisdom he has given us. God wanted us to think for ourselves; be strong. In closing, we have overcome this hurdle in life, and we did pass the test of life. Thank you, Jesus.

Sometimes, now may not be until tomorrow.
I will always put God first.
I'm glad to be second.

How You Doing

When someone asks you, "How are you doing?" we usually say, "I'm doing fine." Are you really fine? Your tone and expressions tell me that you are not fine. You may be okay, but you need to vent. So talk to me. What's on your mind when I asked you how you are doing? One should never bottle up their feelings, nor should they tell the world how they feel; by that, I mean do not Facebook your problem. By that, I mean the ones reading your problems just do not care how you're doing. Oh, they read it and think, "Glad that's not me." The worst part is when they comment on your problems, they say, "Sorry" and "I hope everything gets better," but in my opinion, they are just commenting on what makes them feel good but does nothing for you. Just looking at their comments makes you more depressed because now it went from your mind (which hopefully you forget your problems) to where you can rehash your problems every time you open your page. So sad. You need to talk to God. He is willing to listen without commenting, and he can and will help you. All this is private, just between you and God. I believe he will tell you to stop dwelling on the bad things and think how beautiful you are and that you belong in his paradise. God and his son Jesus are your *in* for feeling good about yourself and a way *out* of your sadness. Live your life free as your problems have a different meaning now. *(They are not tormenting you anymore.)* Thank God and his son Jesus for making you move forward and not looking back. Smile more for your well-being even if you have to fake a smile, and soon enough, that smile will be genuine.

You should heal those wounds.

Humble

I would like to think that I am a humble person. I don't feel that I am better than anyone. Also, I don't feel like they are better than me. I like to live my life quietly and without a lot of fanfare. A serene environment for me to just lay back and relax. I like to travel to places in my mind that I would like to go in real life; however, I can do that in my own living room. Just me, and I would like to think that I am not the only one who feels this way. I do not brag about my accomplishments because they really belong to Jesus, who made everything I do possible. When I picture him with all his purity, I feel very humble and wish I could be that way. At the start of this, I said I would like to think I'm humble; in the time that I sit here, I realize I am humble. I know this because I do not confuse being humble with being humbled as I know I would never berate anyone. God loves all his people, and through him, I humbly say so do I.

Thank you, Jesus.
Always be glad that you are you.
It works for all that is pure of heart.
Now is better than never.

I Need a Break

I need a break from life. There are so many things that drag me down. Sometimes I feel so depressed, I think I will explode. Haven't you felt that way? I hope not. But if you did and still do, let's figure this out with God's help. I believe we are dwelling on God too much. We need a break from God. Not in our hearts, but in our minds. We need to focus on our lives and our priorities. God is the priority; he and his son (Jesus) are number 1. And we have to let them go for one day. Not in our hearts, but in our minds. We need some time alone, no matter who loves us. We need to block all thoughts from our minds and quit thinking so much. All this do not have to be permanent but only for a short while. You must not give up hope on yourself and please quit feeling sorry for yourself. Your family loves you as does God and his son Jesus. If you don't do this for yourself, then do it for them. Soon, the sun will shine on you, and your heart will feel the warmth; you will look in the mirror and wonder what's different, and that would be you because you are smiling. You realize now you are a strong person and can overcome most anything, and you will start to make wise decisions. One of the main things to remember when you take a break from God is that he was still with you, but clearer now in your mind. Above all, now you can thank him for your new life without the anchor.

In reference, St. Dominic went through this because of his love for God and couldn't help people become Christians by himself.

"I have met with my enemies, and now they want to be friends."

I replied, "I do not wish to be your friend nor do I wish to be your enemy."

Inequity

We go through our life trying to be fair. We try to be fair in our treatment to others. We try to be fair in our dealings with our neighbors. Life would be so nice and peaceful if only our neighbors felt the same. No inequities. There seems to be no justice in our minds about how we are treated. Life seems to work for the nonbelievers more than the believers. Not so. Our God is there for us, and if we honestly believe the world is against us, we have to change our thoughts and let Jesus lead us. If we continue to believe that, this inequity, we are on a path that leads nowhere. A path we chose and not Jesus. Step back, and ask Jesus for help. He will be there for you and me. We must believe that with all our heart. Jesus is the only true friend we have because he would never lead us anywhere we chose not to go. Jesus loves us when we feel adequate in our travels; he does not want us to lose sight of him regardless of all the inequities. Let's change adequate to really getting fair treatment and not just barely being treated fair. Our mind is now on the path to our destiny because we now believe we are being treated fairly, and we cleansed our mind of all inequities, thanks to Jesus and our God. We are finally free from our thoughts. Be happy for others. And smile more.

New day, same life, better outlook.

Intentions

What are your intentions? That is the question you should ask yourself. You know you do things that you don't mean to do. But you think your intensions are good. Maybe they are in your eyes; in someone else's maybe it did not work out for them. Oh well, my intention was good. Learn to listen very intently to what God has to say. When you do and follow God's rules, you will do the right things positively on purpose. Not just try, as you will succeed in all that you intend to do. God knows you mean well, and he also knows your intentions. He knows your intentions were to go to church. He knows you meant to praise your children and your friends; most of all, he knows you meant to pray when things go well, not just when things do not go well. He knows you meant to thank him for all he gave to you and not for what you would wish he would do for you. God watches over us and tries to guide us down the path he wants us to go. In our mind, our intentions were good.

I can read minds if you don't scribble.
It works for all that is pure of heart.
Now is better than never.

Interview

For me, it's true; only me and God know me. When I was in my earlier years, a priest told me I reminded him of one of the saints. Years later, I could not remember what saint or even if he said, so I began to research the travels of the saints, and when I got to Simon Peter, I was looking at my life. In real life, I am not a saint—at times, far from it. I have always believed in God and tried to get others to feel as I do; however, I do not wish to lead you, I want you to follow God on your own. In my *book Only You and God Know You*, I try to reach all people with an open mind on how to find God. I like to think of my letters as a compass. Especially the last two directions, which is up or down, helping someone to go in the right direction. As I said in my second book, *"I will gladly meet you halfway if I knew where to start."* Keep in mind, if you're looking for God, you're lost; he isn't. *My third book is meant to be my views of the way life progressed.* The letters I write are meant for me, and I want to share them with whoever wishes to have a happier life and make others happy. Don't wait until tomorrow for your life to begin; start now. I don't want to have to sneeze before you bless me. If you like the letters, tell your friends if you don't tell your enemies.

God bless all of you.
Author

Intuition

From the time I was born and able to think for myself, I knew there was a god. And I knew my beliefs were real. As I grew older, I was more and more in need of Jesus. I have to believe I know what is in store for me in the future. I and we have to rely on our instincts to travel the right path that will eventually lead to our destiny. My instinct is to believe that God will fulfill all my dreams. I would like to believe I have the intuition to see that others whoo may not have the instinct that I have need my help. I see they are in need of things even before they realize it. I will give them what I can afford before they ask because no matter how bad they are, they are in need. The good ones have pride in themselves, so asking comes very hard. Let us help our God to help others, and when we do, we shouldn't need them to thank us over and over. A simple smile and a thank-you will suffice.

Let me help carry that burden.
It works for all that is pure of heart.
Now is better than never.

Is This You?

I hope this isn't me. My hopes are to be the person my mother and father raised me to be—with love and mostly understanding. I am very disappointed in me to myself. I know this is not me. Every time I try to be me, something or someone seems to get in my way. It is very humiliating, and I get down on myself, and I feel I am not worthy of God to help me. So sad. If I just had the strength to fight for myself, I feel I could be okay and not be led down the path that I am trying to avoid. Not only do I ask God to help me find what I feel is keeping me from being me, I am also asking for forgiveness even though I feel that I'm not doing anything wrong. Because it's all in my mind—my weaknesses and my ability to help myself, especially my thoughts of being weak. I am trying very hard to be me. And I know in my heart I am a good person. And *I will not let anyone* drag me down ever again. I am not you; I am proud to be me.

The tears I shed are for my broken heart.
It works for all that is pure of heart.
Now is better than never.

It Is What It Is?

We start out with our lives knowing nothing. In our younger years, we have the strength and stamina to do almost anything, especially in our minds. As we get older, we slowly lose some of our strength. When we get to our retirement age, we seem to forget some things, and we are starting to lose some of our stamina. As we reach our seventies, we start to ache. We seem to drop things more. We make many unnecessary trips because we forgot what we went after. No, it's not our lack of memory, and there is nothing wrong with us, only a lack of concentration. This is where we need God to help control our thinking, but we also have to help ourselves. How do you say it? It's impossible because I tried. Well, you have to just try harder, such as clear your head of useless thoughts such as my days are numbered. I'm overwhelmed. Don't keep revisiting those thoughts because it is what it is. Think young thoughts as if it is the beginning. And stop worrying about the children. Trust in God. Slow down. Wait, that's no answer. Try this. Don't blame everything on age as we dropped things all our lives. It's more pronounced now because we hurt a little to bend or stoop over. It didn't bother us then, so why let it bother us now? Life will never be the same, so quit feeling sorry for yourself. Your life is not as bad as you make it out to be. Look in the mirror and give a genuine smile. And I guarantee you, you will receive the same smile right back at you. It also works when you smile at someone. God is proud of you, so be proud of yourself.

Jesus is not only a way out but a way in.

Letters

Someone once very close to me asked, "Why do you write these letters?" Here's why: My goal is to get anyone who is willing to keep an open mind on how to believe in God and believe in Jesus, his son, who died for us. If I can reach just one person, I feel I have done what I accomplished to do; however, if that one person can convince another person or two. I would have done my job even better. And those people tell others, "Well, you get my drift." It would be like a snowball coming down a mountain and turning into an avalanche (I hope) and not only would I have accomplished my goal; it also helped you and others like you. I feel it is our goal in life to better our lives and the lives of all people, regardless of whether they believe or not. Some just do not realize the happiness and rewards it brings into their lives. Believing is like a deep breath and a sigh of relief. *Take a moment to think about it.* Your happiness is in your hands and yours alone. You should never push your beliefs on anyone. I know I have never done that. What I do is back off and let God handle it; after all, he is the boss. What I do after that is I say a prayer for them and me.

I believe in God also I believe in me.
It works for all that is pure of heart.
Now is better than *never.*

Life Stinks

What are your thoughts for today? You say, "Same as yesterday and same as this morning." I wonder why that is? Could it be the same routine day after day? Could it be you are thinking way too much? So many questions. Maybe that's it. You question life as it is today and how it was yesterday and probably how it will be tomorrow. Why's that? Are you afraid to let go of yesterday, and it carries on until tomorrow and the day after and the days after that? Why is that? Are you afraid to face life, or are you thinking about the beyond? Life is a question mark. Life is how you perceive it. Don't be afraid of life; embrace it. Do you feel like you missed something in life? So what? It probably wouldn't change your thoughts anyway. It may be you are thinking too much; that's a common thing, but you must control your thinking. You can do it on your own. Be happy who you are. God is pleased with you. That's really all that matters in life. When you face another day, wake up with a smile on your face. Then maybe, just maybe, life won't seem so bad as for you to say, "Life stinks." Remember, people love you as you are. Don't change a thing except your composure.

Limited Love

Always something new. Limited love is not one of those things. You can limit yourself to the amount of food you eat. You can limit the time you do things. All about a person's limit to do what they please. Let's stop and think, what if the limitation is not just about you? What if your wife or husband is needing more than your limit to them? Not only does this limitation apply to you, it also applies to your other half. When you crave something/anything, and there is only very little of it, and you are not satisfied and you want more, so you get frustrated when there is no more. Yes, I am talking about affection between husband and wife. When you and your other half feel fulfilled, the affection slows down, and that's what God planned for love for the both of you. When one of the partners seems to avoid affection before the grace period ends, problems arrive. Sometimes, one of the halves avoids a real kiss because they believe it will lead to affection; this is where one or the other seems they have to find someone else (*in their mind*). Hence, an affair starts. Not because they fell out of love, but because their love for their mate was limited. Let's also keep in mind the grace period may take less time and sometimes a little longer (grace period is approximately two years before you both settle down with each other and get on with your Christian life). Talk about it so you both understand instead of forming your own opinion about limited love. By doing that, intimacy should never ever be outside of your marriage for either person. Not God's way. Nor should be yours.

Lost

I have been waiting for Christmas to write this because it is the day our savior was born, as it was, then it will be now; nothing's changed where Jesus is concerned. He will continue to watch over you. I don't mean going to church. I always look at church as a starting place to keep our lives on course. You and I are past that stage; it's like believing in God in our hearts so we can be exempt from this. No, I don't mean forever, but for now (*going to church*). We must rely on our hearts and minds to guide us with Jesus's help. Church will also help when you are ready. Sometimes, we feel that there is no hope or a fresh start. *Those are myths.* A person with your intelligence must try to understand the ones that are not as fortunate as you. You are not only book smart, but you are also street smart—that gives you an edge. With all that being said, let's slow down and let the less fortunate try to catch up. While we do this, we must know that all our sins have been forgiven by the *sacrifice of Jesus on the cross.* So we *must not* judge others; God knows we've been judged by others who are less intelligent. That's why we should overlook the mistakes of others. *God will judge them.*

When you are comfortable with yourself, you will begin to feel the freedom within and go to church. Happiness will come naturally. There is not a moment when Jesus is not on my mind twenty-four hours a day; that is where I get my street smarts. *You know what to do.* All that is left is to put love in your heart and act naturally; you already know how to say I love you. Now believe it and show it—of course at your own pace. *The world is not ugly;* it's some of the things in this world that has taken the luster out of it. Don't let that sway you; you are *so beautiful/handsome.* When I look at you, I have to smile and be thankful you are my *grandchild.* We all would like the things to be as they were, but they are not, but *they could be.* We have to take a moment to look at our lives now and what our lives could be.

Even bad things come to an end.
Let today be the start of your life.
I believe in God; also I believe in me.
You can live your normal life and still love God.
Thinking ahead, see you all in church.

Motivation

Sometimes we feel like we should just lay around and do nothing. Sometimes that is exactly what we need to do. We are not ready to face the world or all its challenges. That is when we become overwhelmed with how to do things. If only God gave me the strength to get motivated. It seems I cannot do it myself or maybe I don't feel like it, or I am simply just lazy. Who knows? I will tell you, who knows. You know. And God already knew. And he will help to get you motivated. I feel he will tell you it's in your mind the way you think. As we all know, when we accomplish our tasks, we feel very good about ourselves. Then the world doesn't seem so bad. When we get motivated and feel like we are full of energy, we get things done. Now that we are motivated, thanks to our God, we should pray and give thanks. Two ways to pray with our built-in cross: Entwine your fingers or simply put your hand together. Either way, make a cross with your thumbs. And picture Jesus on that cross. *Instant motivation.*

If I knew then what I know now, I still wouldn't know.
It works for all that is pure of heart.
As of now, I'm still human.
Now is better than never.

My Battle

From the time I was born, I could remember I was always in a battle between good and evil (aka God and Satan). Sometimes it was so hard to tell the difference. I would listen to my thoughts and reset them to the way I think. Sometimes I would make a mistake and then realize it was Satan interfering in my life and telling me what to do. I only wish I knew ahead of time who was trying to lead me. My life would be so simple. Life is not that easy to tell the difference, and that is where my heart steps in and tells my conscience whether it is good or bad. I then thank God I was able to overcome the voice in my head that it was Satan, not God, trying to lead me. I thank God again that he gave me the ability to follow him (Jesus) as my life was always holy. Thank you, Jesus, for telling your father that I am a good man. Being human, I make mistakes, but I thank God and his son that the mistakes I make can be corrected as they were of no harm to anyone but me. My concern is I wish I could win this battle, but I realize this battle goes on. Thank you, Jesus, I know you will never give up on me. I will travel the path that leads me to you.

Hail Mary, full of grace, the Lord is with you.
It works for all that is pure of heart.
Now is better than never.

My Birthday

Here is another year and another birthday. Am I looking forward to the next birthday? Absolutely, and if I may, I will tell you why. Let's start with my saying I love you very much and every day of my existence, I look forward to waking up and knowing you are there for me. I realize it is a full-time thing taking care of me, not because you think I need being taken care of, but because of the love and understanding we have between us. I try to be the best person that I can. And suffice it to say, sometimes I fall short of that goal. I do try very hard to keep things in order. Again, I fall short of that goal. That is another reason I look forward to my next birthday, not because of me, but because of you. And I thank you, God, and your son Jesus for my time on Earth to spend with you and my wife. I love you.

I believe in God, and also, I believe in me.
I have enough time to live; I don't have to borrow any.
With all my love, Judith, your husband Jerry

Now You Know

As I lay here in bed, I began to think. I hate doing that (thinking) at night when I should be giving thanks to God and his son Jesus and getting my sleep time in without worrying about anything. The reason I started thinking was in the last few days of my life, it was very hectic. Overwhelming, I should say. A certain amount of confusion. So in my mind, I started thinking about God and Satan. When it came to me thinking about God, I asked a few questions (*to God*) such as, why is this burden on me? I know I am special to you, and I called your name for answers. I did receive your answer, and it was short and to the point. The answer was "Man up and quit being sorry for yourself." So now what? (*I expected more.*) I spent some time with Satan in my past and younger years. Don't fear; it was nothing really bad because Jesus would step in. Sometimes, it was a close call. I don't like bringing up the past as it just brings back bad memories. With that being said, I called upon Satan to get some answers. I felt I had earned the right to communicate with Satan, so I asked, "Why?" I said, "When I traveled with you, you knew my heart was with God. Why are you trying to get back in my life? We parted ways on friendly terms. I did what you asked to a certain point. So again why now?"

"The answer I got was I (Satan) can keep promises too. It is not me, it's you. It's you thinking about the past. I even sent one of my angels to let you know that, but you would not receive my angel. Your reason in your mind was because you felt an evil presence. It is you, not me. You should take God's advice and man up to your own mind. So as I hope you understand it's not God, and it's not me (Satan). Keep in mind I have more followers than I had before your time. I really don't need you at this point in time. I'm glad to hear from you, but you are always welcome here. Sorry, Jerry, I had to try to win you back. And thanks for praying to your God for me. I have the power, but it is wasted on losers. And sometimes that's how I feel

when I leave your God. My days are good, I mean bad, and maybe
one day, God will have his utopia."

You can be friends with whomever you please,
but you do not have to be a follower.
Love and understanding life.

Nuisance

Why do I sometimes feel out of place in this world? Like I belong in another time or place. My generation from the time I was born to the present time changed so much, or maybe the times didn't change; maybe I did. I am terribly uncomfortable in these times. Sometimes I feel like I'm a burden to society. I know in my heart I truly am not. But I sometimes feel like I'm a nuisance to others when in reality, I am a kind and compassionate person, just the way God wanted me to be. I love most all people and most things in life, so why can't I convince myself? Why do I feel this way? Hold on for a minute; I have to have an internal talk with Jesus. Jesus said to me I should man up and not take life so seriously. He also said I should smile more. I do not need to pray that I am a nuisance to anyone and just accept the fact that it is only in my mind. So I will take Jesus's advice and simply man up.

Imaginary pain hurts as bad as physical pain.
It works for all that is pure of heart.
Now is better than never.

Oh No

Here it is, another birthday for Jesus. I turned on the television hoping to hear someone singing, "Happy birthday, Jesus." I searched over a couple of hundred channels to see if someone was out there celebrating his birthday. I could not find one. What I did find was many vulgar networks with no hesitation or bleeps, saying the most foul language you could hear. Also, many of the channels were of a sexual nature. No, I am not without sin, but my sins are committed when I smack my hand with a hammer. It is not my everyday language as it is for some. Also, remember your children are watching what I just experienced. Don't think for a minute when they tell you they are not watching. Not only them but their classmates do the same as well. Can you imagine a seven-year-old saying those words?

Well, they are; just ask your child (*if you are a Christian yourself*). So I tried to look at his birthday in another way, as this world is getting harder and harder to understand. I looked for signs on television of Merry Christmas. There were none to find. I looked in the newspaper, also nothing. I'm beyond trying to find out what is going on in today's world. Oh, I see many well-known channels saying "Happy holidays." And the signs saying, "Merry Xmas." What is going on? Are we too weak to stand up for our savior Jesus Christ, our leader, who can destroy his creation in a heartbeat? I personally will say "Merry Christmas" to you whether you like it or not. You must remember there will be a time when you (your soul) will stand in front of God. Be sure you have your excuses with you. I'm talking about *you* who lets this happen in my country and yours. Oh no, it is too late for you to make up any excuse. No luck with Jesus. Try his neighbor; he loves your kind.

Oppression

We should always live our lives free. God made his freedom for you and for you to be free, no matter who you are. Some people and some countries try to oppress you and our country. We sometimes have to fight for our freedom. Wouldn't it be wonderful if all countries made it a law to not be oppressive? Whereas we should not have been oppressed in the first place. Domination over us should never happen in God's paradise. Even in a marriage, one may feel like they can and should rule over the other whether it be the man, the woman, or the child. Listen to God; he will make you equal and try to make you understand life. You will then love your family as a unit, all for one. Sometimes we do not get along with our neighbors over silly things; closeness seems to do that. As I always say, the worst people living next to you are neighbors, and no one should feel that way. Try to get along; do not be oppressive to anyone. God says love your neighbor as a family; he did not mean individually. Sometimes we feel oppressed even when we are not. That's called a chip on your shoulder or simply being misled and misinformed. Free yourself so that you may free others.

Skip the sarcasm and just pretend to be friends.
It works for all that is pure of heart.
Now is better than never.

Perception

W hat is our perception of life? We know we cannot see into the future for ourselves or others. Only God can give us the ability to think about how life can be. We all know how we would like it to be. So why don't we work to make our lives better? It is not out of the realm of possibilities. It can come to pass as we perceive it. We can picture Adam and Eve in God's paradise without a care in the world. No neighbors to bother you. No waiting in line at the supermarket. Only their paradise. Freedom to enjoy what God gave them. If only they had a little perception of their future, they would have left that fruit alone. We live in a world where there are too many rules. They lived in a world where God only gave them one rule (not to eat the apple). Again, we can't blame them. We probably would have done the same thing. I mean, break a few rules. I understand their rule came from God. Ours came from man. With all that said, God had the perception to know how we would be. He gave us rules that were only good for us. And Jesus, his son, died so we can live free. God had the perception to see that we would sin as did Adam and Eve, so he threw in safeguards—one being the perception to forgive us for our sins.

I will always put God first.
It works for all that is pure of heart.
Now is better than *never.*

Premarriage

It seems like forever for you to meet the right person for you. You go to different functions thinking you will meet the perfect match for you. It may, but it may not. Sometimes, let fate and God take a hand in this. You may not want to go to a certain function and decide as a last thought to go and meet your one and only. This relationship should not include just the two of you; it must include both sides of your families. Try to understand your future mother-in-law's actions because she wants the best for her son (which is you) and the father-in-law because he thinks he's losing his little girl. Be patient whether you be the female or the male. Think your thoughts out, and if they are negative, keep them to yourself, and if they are positive, don't be afraid to speak. Don't pretend to be the likable person that you are. And thank God that you remained calm. First impressions do matter. And yes, they can grow into something beautiful. Don't create a problem. Also, an engagement is not a license for intimacy. Don't be pressured into something you may regret. After marriage is when you both enjoy life as God intended. Please try to understand each other's ways. And talk to each other to work out any little problems that may arrive; love and life will endure forever, and there will be many smiles in your home. The engagement time is for you to get to know one another. Don't spill your guts, but be fair, and if you trust your future mate, they will understand, and the weight on your mind should be lighter now. Before you do, make sure you haven't tried God first. Then maybe God will free you from the past if you are troubled and free you from details you only should know.

Rapture

Just once I would like to have rapture in my life. Oh, I have my times of joy, but that joy only seems to last a short while. Sometimes, not even a day. I try to smile when others are around because I try with all my heart not to drag them down. Because I'm pretty sure they would like to have rapture in their lives. Some may not. I hope not. We all seem to be preoccupied with something. Sometimes that something won't go away. It may be your job, or it may be a project you're working on, or it may be a legal problem. Nevertheless, it keeps you thinking. It is hard to control your thinking. We have to try to block out the bad and have happy thoughts. No, I am not fantasizing this can really happen with God's help. Everything you do with God's help turns to happiness and just maybe you can find your rapture in God. That's my plan for the future. And I am delighted to tell you I am looking forward to my overwhelming happiness in God. Nothing else matters. I will be happy and wait patiently for my rapture to come. And some day, it will. You can bet on that because God is your sure bet to overwhelming happiness, and nothing else matters.

Read between the Lines

I'm reasonably sure we all heard that when we didn't get the point, or maybe we just didn't understand what was being said to us. Maybe we did understand what we heard, but it was only meant to go so far. Am I confusing you? Well, I meant to. If you're confused about what I said in the above, you are not reading between the lines. A lot of salespeople or just ordinary people speak at a louder tone or may say something not related to what their selling or saying. That is so you lose your train of thought on the product they are selling. Their tone is nonstop, so you can't follow everything that is being presented to you. Somewhere along the line, we should say, "Hold on. I'm trying to follow you." If you read the Bible, there are so many things being said that it is impossible for you to come to the same conclusion about the same thing you have all read. God knows what he said, and his words are clear. Yet there are some making what is said, a different meaning (that's called reading between the lines). Try to look at things in your eyes as I believe someone said you can only believe what you see for yourself. That is true to a certain point because sometimes you see, but you are blind to what you see. I know what I'm saying because I see it every day. Some people say things to you that they know you're bound to find out. Those things are called half-truths. Not the whole story, and that is so at a later time in life, you do find out, and their answer to you would be, "I told you so."

You didn't read between the lines.
Pay attention when I'm talking to you.

Reincarnation

This is a very controversial subject. The reason being is that some religions do not believe you will return to Earth in a new body. That's okay. The body means nothing; it houses your soul. The soul is yours forever. There is nothing written in stone about this. The pro side of coming back (your soul) is we all make mistakes, and sometimes we feel like only death will release those mistakes. This is not true; life will erase all mistakes if only we keep an open mind and try harder to believe you can be forgiven. God made you. One scenario is you will stay in heaven or hell. Even heaven or hell can be overcrowded. Another scenario is we have a chance in this life to improve what we couldn't in our previous life. Complicated? No, even without reincarnation, you should improve your life. Another scenario is if we have only one life. Why don't we live to be two hundred or more years of age? That is unrealistic because our bodies would shrink to the point of being unrecognizable. Only God knows. We are not on the same level as God or his son Jesus; they are at the top of the mountain, but we are God's children, and we should try to reach God by how high we can climb God's mountain in this life (our morals). However, what we do know is Jesus came back to life. Some of the religions believe we will not come back simply because other religions say we will come back. Grudges not only interrupt their lives; they also interrupt ours. You must believe in your thoughts. The road you travel and your mountain to climb. In my world, pantheism is true. You must always remember; my soul will always be me, and your soul will always be you whether you believe in reincarnation or not.

PS: I can hold a grudge longer than anyone I know, and that grudge is that I am still unhappy with the doctor that slapped me when I was born.

Revelations

We sometimes wonder if we will ever get to the point where we can just relax and be happy. We have to make our own happiness with our hearts and minds. If you are constantly thinking about the bad things, your brain won't release those thoughts, so they go on day after day. What I try to do is just simply don't go there. As soon as my thinking goes awry, I change my thought process by thinking of something good. Surprisingly, it does work. When you trust in God, one day you will wake up, and you will be surprised at your new life. Surprise others with your newfound identity. They will be so surprised at the way you see them and the world in a new light. Thanks to God. God is full of unexpected surprises as to what he can do for you and others who seem to be stuck in one place. Accept God's offer to make a better world for yourself; it's there. Just do it and take the offer. You deserve to be happy and relaxed. When you at least try, there will be no bad revelations. Surprise yourself.

You can get there from here.
It works for all that is pure of heart.
Now is better than never.

Righteousness

Everyone behaves in a different way. We all see things the way we perceive them to be. It may be that another person sees the same thing we saw, but their opinion is different than ours. As we all know, opinions vary. That's all well and good if your opinion is about ordinary things; however, when it is a matter of being righteous, opinions should not vary. We all think in our minds we are right about what we say and think. And as I said, opinions vary. Well, it should not vary when we believe and trust in God and his son Jesus. There is no varying in this case. Right is right. God's righteousness is beyond reproach. Being right does not make you righteous. God makes you righteous. You only have to believe in God and follow the path to righteousness that he has laid out for you. When you think you're right and you believe you won the debate that you were having with someone, only to find out you were wrong. It doesn't feel all that good to be wrong. Because if you're a righteous person, you will go to the other party you were debating and say, "I'm sorry. I was wrong, and you were right." (Saying you're sorry is not a sign of weakness in this case.) Not only have you released the guilt feeling, your mind is also clearer. You are now on your way to being one of God's children as you always were; now you feel like you are no longer the black sheep of the family (God's family). You believe you are one of God's children and on your way to being righteous in your eyes and God's.

Being honorable and loving and righteous makes for a good night of sleep and pretty dreams.

Rosary

There is so much power in the rosary. It should be used in all religions as it is the biography of our Lord Jesus. We won't use the word (story) because it is not a story at all. It is all facts and should never be disputed by anyone; even the devil would not go there. It has many familiars, especially the Hail Marys. No matter how many times you say the Hail Mary, it is never enough as it forgives us for our sins. It tells of Jesus's journey through his life, and it shows all his travels from birth to the crucifixion. I believe he had the same life as we live, as his father wanted him to see the way people lived (you and me). The only difference, I believe, is that we had our ups and downs. For Jesus, after the teen years, I don't suppose he had much ups, only downs. He was in battle for us. He is still fighting our battles. We should give Jesus all the praise that he rightly deserves. His path was always clear; ours was not.

If you reach out, my hand will be there.
It works for all that is pure of heart.
Now is better than never.

Rotation

You heard the adage: You can't take it with you, that's true, but it will be there when you return to your new life. That's what it means when they say he or she was born with a silver spoon in their mouth. Another thing in your new life, *If you turn out in your mind to be a nonbeliever in God and his Son Jesus*, things could change. Maybe you started out a couple of lifetimes ago and were very successful, and now you are not. Hard to understand? Let's make it easy; your ego that lived in your previous life got greedy and didn't realize how he or she got that fortune that he or she is about to lose. Even if you were born into it, it's now your place to recover the losses of your past; to do that, you must believe in God and his son Jesus as did your soul in previous times. (*That's how the fortune amassed.*) He (God) does not want you to go backward; he wants you to be successful. When they say your past will catch up to you, that's what they mean. Another adage is you can't get there from here—nonsense. You can if you know where to start. *Too hard to understand!* Ask God to meet you halfway and then you can get there from there. Be generous with what you have; by that, I don't mean give everything you have away. Don't miss the point I am trying desperately to make to you. Never deny food to the hungry; if you are aware of who is hungry, feed them. When I say grace my way, I ask God to feed the hungry. God is our savior, but you have to be worthy of his commandments. If you break a commandment (keep in mind there are only ten), ask God to forgive you and sin no more.

Imaginary pain hurts as bad as physical pain.
If not for the bad things, how would we know the good things?

Salt of the Earth

What does salt of the Earth really mean? I believe it means when you have no religion or religious beliefs, you are not the salt of the Earth. God wants you as an individual to believe in him and also believe what he does. Just think of an ocean liner traveling the oceans without any forms or means of direction. The captain would have no idea where he/she is heading without a compass and a map to let he/she know which directions to point the liner in. I'm talking about the present times, not the past times when the stars were placed by God to let you know all the directions. Most people believe God made only four directions: north, south, east, and west. That is not so in my opinion. I believe we are leaving out the two most important directions that decide our fate in life, and they are up and down. You simply cannot go through life as a vagabond. (*If you believe in your life as a vagabond, so be it. I am not here to judge.*) You must trust and believe in God to lead you in the right direction. His directions will keep you safe from getting lost in life and travel the path he (God) paved for you. Have you noticed lately that you don't seem to smile as you did when you were younger? That's because you somehow got off the path that God chose for you and you alone, your path in life. In order for you to be the salt of the Earth, you must do two things: Number 1 is to believe and praise our God, not sometimes but every waking moment. Please understand I believe God does not want to confuse you by saying think of him only; he wants you to go through your life smiling, and secondly, seeing the light he has lit for you to see his world. If you can be honest with yourself and you do the right things in God's eyes, you are the salt of the Earth.

Undeniably.
Everything seems to come naturally when you make it a habit.

Satan

*S*atan is a scary word. Why do you suppose that is? There are other words that are scary such as *danger, watch out, boo*. To make a point, we should not be afraid of words. We know those things are real, but they are still words. Words will only hurt our feelings, so ignore most things, but just to be on the safe side, watch out for those things. No, I don't mean to expect them, just be aware of them. Life is sometimes scary enough on its own. Don't look for things to happen; just thank Jesus for helping to avoid those traps without us even knowing we were in danger. Thank you, Jesus. I like to live my life free and to go on serving you. I need your help to guide me in the direction you would take as my life and death belongs to you and only you.

If not for the bad things, how would we know the good things?
It works for all that is pure of heart.
Now is better than never.

Senior Day

We miss the days that you were here with us while you were growing up to be the outstanding young man/woman that you are. We are proud and happy that you chose us to be your grandparents. We think of you and your sisters/brothers all the time. I try to remember the times (*grandson*) when you had your first baseball game. That was when you were seven or eight. Wait, wait, I just remembered, and now I'm trying to forget because you liked rolling around in the outfield in those days. Even then I was so proud of you. In high school, you made up for the little league. Hey, sis, I didn't forget about you even though ladies first. You belong on a pedestal then and now. You blossomed into a beautiful person. I hope now you see why we had to drag you to the dance studio and piano lessons. Now it's your time to take care of your sisters/brothers, love and protect them from life's dangers. You will be going on life's journey on your own now, but you won't really be alone because the path that you choose will be supported by gram and me, so anywhere that you are, we will be there with you and for you.

Just because you can't see it doesn't mean it's not there.
Love and prayers,
Mom and Dad
Gram and Papa

Serenity

Sometimes, life is very troubling; we feel distressed and uncomfortable. Why is that? In my mind, I think way too much about my problems, and they are not huge, just too many. What I need to do is to calm down and not feel so distressed. In other words, be serene; mellow out. Leave the worrying for another day; let today be bright and comfortable for me and you. No clouds in my world or yours today, only sunshine. I will definitely stay calm and not think about my troubles, not today, and I hope I am strong enough to include tomorrow and hopefully the rest of the week and the weeks and months to come. In short serenity now and forever for us. God will keep us serene as always, but we have to believe in him (*God the father and Jesus his son*) and ourselves to carry out his plan for us, and that is to be happy. We should keep smiling. What I do is to picture Jesus's mother Mary and say the Hail Marys over and over until I see Mary clearly in my images. Serenity now and forever. Thank you, Jesus.

Love sometimes does come easy.

Singularity

We are one of many. We are so different from one to the other. Some of us love others and will do everything we can within our limits to make others happy. Then there is the other side of the coin. People who purposely go out of their way to make our lives uncomfortable. Yes, I said uncomfortable, not miserable as we are strong enough to overcome anything they have to offer. We can make our lives miserable, but they cannot. Why do you think life is that way? Or maybe you don't think that. Again, singularity. Your option to think for yourself in all matters of life. You make your choices the way you want weather your on one side of the coin or the other side. God gave you that right, but you are the one who has to live with the decisions you make. Oh yes, you can blame others for your shortcomings, and that may satisfy you and you alone. Again, singularity.

You and you alone must take command of your life and make the choices that is easier for you to live with. And make your acquaintances in life easier in the process. Do you know why I used the word *acquaintances* instead of *friends*? You really don't know your friends and believe it or not, you don't want to know them. Here's why: The more you know about a person, the more you will drift apart from them. Just let them live their life and you, yours. Again, singularity. God made us to think for ourselves. He did not make everyone to think alike. That's a good thing. God made us to think beautiful thoughts and put beauty in our bodies and minds. He made us to love, not hate; that is Satan's description to make our life a turmoil, not God's. Our world and life would be so wonderful if there was only one side to the coin and we all loved each other, and that includes all races and all nations in God's world. Let's stick to reality; there will always be two sides to every coin. One side is laughter, and the other is sadness. You alone pick the side that fits you. God wants you in his life.

My life is a story yet to be told.

Solitude

One should never be alone. It may be by choice or maybe people just can't be around you. No matter what the case is, we should always be around people. If we are alone all the time, we get irritated and frustrated. Yes, we can also get that way around people, but we learn who we can be around with. Being alone, you're one, only you. God did not think that was a good idea when he made Adam. He saw that Adam was lonely, so he made Eve. Adam and Eve were very happy with each other, and Adam finally was able to smile because he now was content with Eve to talk to. And as I always say, two is better than one. It works that way with all of God's creatures. You shouldn't have only one fish in an aquarium. Same for all farm animals; they get lonely too. House animals like dogs need a companion because you are not there 24-7. When you have only one, you see how happy they are when you come home. Same with all humans. So if you enjoy solitude, make sure you have Jesus in your heart; also remember, you don't know what you're missing by being alone, and that is happiness.

If you reach out, my hand will be there.

Soul

We hear a lot of people say, "With all my heart and soul." I wonder if they understand what they said. We know we can give our hearts to someone, but we cannot give our souls to anyone. It is ours; however, it is (spiritually) from God to only you. Your identity in his world. To clarify this, think of your social security card that you were assigned. It is yours for life. You cannot give it away (you can, but that would be a huge mistake). With your soul, you cannot do anything with it. It is there to take notes about you. God's secretary, if you will. It keeps records about only you—everything good and bad and all in between. Why, you ask? Here's why: God needs to know all the facts about you; your personal history, he already knows, but he wants to review them with you so he (God) can decide your fate after death and while you are facing your maker. The truth will come out, as the soul cannot tell a lie or form an opinion.

"I don't understand because I'm not part of your world."

When God sees your life, he will then make a decision on what happiness you deserve in your new life. If you just went through life doing nothing, you may return as you were. If you made a special attempt to better your life in the previous life, you would have a better new life. If God does not like what he sees, you will be turned over to Satan (you will still keep your soul) even in Satan's world. However, you probably won't mind because that is what you did in your previous life. Now in Satan's world, you will do his bidding because now you don't have any choices. In God's world, you made your choices, and see where it landed you. Somewhere along your path, you may realize now how it could have been. I believe in Satan's world, you can still break away from Satan completely with your heart and love of our God. Ask God to forgive you. God still owns your soul, so in another life, after this one, God may reconsider your options, as God is a forgiving God. I hope that works for you. As you waste another lifetime, God will let you start over. Satan can be defeated. God cannot; the choice is yours. Short-term or a life filled with love and joy. Your soul will be with you for all eternity and only end when God sees his creation and creations destroyed by the hand of man. And then, he alone will destroy his paradise.

Somebody does know your thoughts.
Pick a time when you want your life to begin.
It works for all that is pure of heart.
Now is better than *never.*

Spending My Day

I know how I would like to spend my day. Ultimately, it is my choice how to spend my day, but life doesn't always let you be you. It could be a friend you would rather not spend this day with, but you do anyway; that's a day lost. Why is it so hard to just say no? You are hurting yourself. If you do, what you would rather not do instead of what you would rather do? Here's a thought: Satan loves it when you spend the day with him (*and that's what you're doing*) because he knows it makes you feel terrible, which he loves when you are hurting. God understands you sometimes like to just be by yourself. It is not a sin in this case to just say to your friend, "I'd love to, but today, I would rather just be alone." Thanks for understanding, and we will get together soon. Sometimes I just simply take a little stroll around the yard by myself and enjoy my company. Sometimes I would just go for a little drive. And sometimes, I would just have lunch alone. I know when I feel like being by myself, I know Jesus is there watching over me, and that makes me happy and makes me smile. He knows I am just reflexing and getting my thoughts in order and relaxing doing what I want and not pressuring myself, just being myself. And believe me, that is not a waste of time. And I sleep better as I leave today and look forward to tomorrow. Oh, I almost forgot; sometimes after my stroll, I would take a small nap. That keeps me alert. Thank you, Jesus.

My goal is to make me happy.
God is the medicine for your soul.
It works for all that is pure of heart.
Now is better than never.

The Story of Life

These are some of the timelines of the history of God's world as I believe them to be. Let's start with Adam who lived approximately 930 years after being created by God from the dust of God's world. Within six days plus one day of rest, seven days (the time it took God to create his world), Eve was created from one of Adam's rib. The main children of Adam and Eve where Cain, his firstborn, and Abel and Seth, the third. They, Adam and Eve, in their life span had possibly eighteen girls and twenty-two boys. God made Adam and Eve pure, but that did not last long. Now we move on to Noah (whom God chose to build an ark for two of all his creatures). That was approximately, I believe, around 4004 BC. Noah lived I believe approximately 950 years. And Noah had three sons, Shem, Ham, and Japeth, whom God wanted to be the means to repopulate the Earth. God wanted them to go in different directions after the flood with their wives. They had, I believe, other plans; so they went against God's wishes and built a tower so they could have their own route to heaven. The tower was to be as high to reach the heavens. And I believe this is when different cultures started and different languages started because they made God angry.

God eventually sent them in different directions. Let's move on to Moses, who came into the picture approximately 1,377 years after Noah. Moses was born approximately 1593 BCE and lived, I believe, approximately 120 years, so with that said, it was, I believe, approximately 2,500 years from Adam to Moses. After God had Moses lead his people out of Egypt, they wandered around for forty years. Then God sent Moses to the mountain to receive his Ten Commandments. God was very disappointed in the way the world was from Adam to Moses, and that is (in my opinion) why God said to himself, "Enough is enough."

During that period, from Adam to Noah to Moses, all the Ten Commandments were broken many times over, although at that time in history, God did not have the Ten Commandments in play. In his mind, he (God) did from the beginning of his creations. It was to be his utopia. So sad the way things conspired. I believe he decided to spell it out to his people. At this time, God set guidelines for the future. One race of people is made up of different ethnics. All started with Adam and Eve and will eventually end up with us. Starting with this generation, 2024, let's all help each other to give God his utopia as our thanks for giving us life. We cannot be perfect, but we can all respect one another, which is what we all want and need, and spread God's word. Let us make our own history in God's world by being the best in our timeline of being respectful to our creator. Let the future historians talk about us as being closest to God in all the previous years of history. Let us have theological virtues. Let us be a nation of one God.

Study and live by God's commandments, and
you will receive many rewards from God.

Summation of the Rosary

The rosary consists of Our Fathers and Hail Marys and has been around for centuries. Around 1214, when the church began to do the rosary, it was presented to the church by St. Dominic, and he got it from Mary. Backing up, St. Dominic wanted to save the world by making it sinless, but he did not know how. I believe he prayed for several days and cried for knowledge of what he couldn't do. He almost lost his life doing so. Then Mary told St. Dominic the rosary, in my belief, is your most valuable possession (my words). St. Dominic tried preaching the rosary to the sinners around the world, hopefully converting them to Christianity. During the course of his teachings, he had to fight much resistance, probably by Satan. St. Dominic preached in his way and wasn't exactly as Mary wanted it, so she told him what to say, and that was in Paris. So I believe after a century or so, in his preaching the rosary, St. Dominic kinda put the cart in front of the horse, as the saying goes, and Satan saw his chance and convinced people away from the rosary. This was around 1349, and God almost destroyed his creations in several countries at this time, which went on for many years.

After that, Mary and Jesus told blessed Alan Laroche during one of his sermons to preach the rosary. It seems that as Alan bulked somewhat at the idea and was scolded harshly by Jesus, telling him (Alan) that he was crucifying me (Jesus) again. Alan did not understand what he did wrong. So Jesus straightened him out. And the rosary was revived. The people through God named it rosary (crown of roses). Later at some point in time, Mary said that every time you say the Hail Mary, she would give you a rose to make the crown of roses. The whole rosary consists of five decades of chaplets (small beads), fifty-three in all and five larger beads, and 153 white roses and sixteen red roses, I believe. The cross is the beginning of saying the rosary, make the sign of the cross, and with the first bead (large bead), recite the Our Father. The next three beads, say the Hail Mary, and in next second large bead, say the Glory Be to the Father. Next is the ten Hail Marys. Next, for the third large bead (first mystery), the Our father then ten more Hail Marys. Large bead (second mystery), ten Hail Marys (third mystery). Please do your homework on the rest until you have completed the circle. You won't be sorry you did. Also, you will be satisfied with yourself for what you accomplished.

Testing

As I said before, we are being tested every day of our lives. Question is, who is doing the testing? Is it Satan trying his best to bring us over to his side? Maybe. Or is it God to see if we are loyal to him? I think it is probably both. I feel like I am being singled out and being overly tested daily. I know in my heart I should get at least a grade of ninety-five. God knows my every thought, and he can verify what I am saying. I suppose the testing will continue, and I hope I can pass most challenges of life. While I'm trying to understand why all this added pressure is put on me, I begin to realize I am being singled out. I am being put through this extensive testing because I believe God knows I am very special, and he needs me to continue my loyalty to him, which I will always do. We need material things to survive. God will supply those needs, but only those needs while living in his paradise. My dream is to wake up one day, for God to tell me the testing is over, and for me to live my life's dream as I see fit. He knows I will not stray. Satan now sees I am not worth his time to pursue me. I am finally free from my thoughts. And with all of life's testing and all the daily pressures, I thank you, Jesus, for finally letting me be me in my final days. Thank you. All my love to all who had this same experience. Stay the course.

For all that is pure of heart.

The following are things not to say around the elderly:

1. Hold it.
2. That depends.
3. Don't fall for that.
4. What do you think?
5. I remember that.
6. Slow down.
7. Hurry up.
8. Could you repeat that?
9. Do you remember when?
10. I didn't sleep well last night.
11. Did you hear that?
12. What's your plan for the future?
13. Do you like steak?
14. How's your legs doing?
15. I will race you to the corner.
16. Did you see that?
17. Help me to remember that.
18. Same time next year.
19. See you soon.
20. Here today, gone tomorrow.
21. I'll miss you.
22. Hang in there.
23. Don't wait for me.
24. Wow, that's old.
25. You're slipping.

Thoughts

I just had a thought. Sometimes that is a good thing if it's controllable. When we think too much, we sometimes lose control of our thoughts. I know I would just like to relax on the sofa and never think about anything or anyone. I have a lot of work to do to control my mind as if it had a mind of its own. When an evil thought comes to mind, think of a word or saying that will get you off that thought. One suggestion is when you have a bad thought, immediately think of Jesus, and it won't hurt to say a couple of Hail Marys. And to make you more comfortable, throw in an Our Father. By then, your mind will be on the good things in life. You can do this with the help of our God. After a short period of time, you may not even have another bad thought. Remember, it's all in your head. Always smile upward because a downward smile is called a frown. Sometimes, I like to get a little silly, but that's just me, and I hope I never change.

I would like to believe I'm living in my world.
It works for all that is pure of heart.
Now is better than never.

Time

That word time is timeless. We go through life every day using the word time without realizing it. We go throughout our day, and we wake up in the night; we look at what time it is. Sometimes we forget the time, and we are late for our appointment. So what do we do? We rush to make up time. If we have time after our appointment, we look at our watch to see if we have time to have dinner. Most of the time we do, but sometimes we don't, but we should make time. After dinner, we saw how much time it took because we had another place to be. There just does not seem to be enough time in the day. Time never seems to stand still during the daylight hours, but at night, when we lay our heads on our pillows and thank God for the good times we had today, time seems to stand still—or at least for eight hours it does. Again, when I start my day, it doesn't seem like I have enough time to do all my chores and make a little private time for myself. Sometimes I like to make time for my loved ones.

Those are my best times and precious times, spending time with my family. My memories will last me a lifetime. Sometimes, after all the rushing around and wasting time, I feel like I must take the time to enjoy my life. Well, I've taken enough time writing this letter about time, so I believe it's time to go. I hope to see you around sometime.

Life is about the good times.
(Jerry Manukin, 08-26-2024)

Tribulation

Life sometimes has its tribulations. We hope we make it through the day or sometimes days without any hardships or distress. Our minds seem to play a little game with us, all the while for us suffering is not a game. Our mind is afflicted by our distress when it may just be a minor problem that's blown way out of proportion. We must learn to control our minds. You say that's impossible because you tried and the same distress signal came along. Be patient and be calm, as getting too exited makes things seem so overwhelmed. Life appears to be a drama with you being the star of this play. So with that said, being the star, take center stage. You being the star, you have a certain amount of say in what's going on. Be in control of your life. Don't make your life more difficult than necessary; relax. You must control your destiny. Don't give in to trials and tribulations. Be strong. You know what you want more than anyone else. So take control of your life as you handle all the drama in a play. Your real life could be controllable and a lot of fun and laughter, so lighten up on yourself. Give yourself a chance. Stop dwelling on the hardships, and soon, you will find out you are free from the past. After this tribulation is over, don't forget to thank Jesus as he guided you through all the emotion and hardship. Sometimes I liken my mind to a magician; it loves to play tricks and illusions on me. So laugh it off as we no longer need your tricks. Make your life enjoyable and forget all the tribulations that life may inflict on you. Then you can be the real you.

You should never feel guilty about good things.
Sometimes I think I'm behind when actually I'm way ahead.

Understanding Satan

Who is Satan, and why do we fear him? Maybe it's the way we were brought up to fear Satan probably. That's okay because in order to keep us humble, we must fear something or someone. Back to Satan, he is just a wayward angel who lost his way. That is why we must not follow him, or we will be lost with him. If I ever get lost, I would like it to be with Jesus as he knows the right path to follow. Satan tried his best to defeat God and his son Jesus not once but twice, and then he realized he was fighting a losing battle, so he went after God's children, and in case you didn't realize, we are God's children—all of us, all races. We should not fear Satan, nor should we follow him. We should pray for Satan and for him to think about how he treated God. I wonder how many times Satan said to himself, "I wish I would have listened to God." It's never too late to come to reality and simply change your ways. I'm talking about me and about Satan. Maybe, just maybe, we can have peace on Earth for all countries and all religions as long as that religion knows we have only one God. No matter how Satan tried, he knows there can only be one God.

Satan has my mouth, but Jesus has my heart.
It works for all that is pure of heart.
Now is better than *never.*

Versatile

Sometimes I feel like I cannot move. I try to stand, but my legs just do not cooperate. I realize I am not as young as I used to be, but I am glad that I'm getting older. That's a good thing; otherwise, I wouldn't be able to communicate with all of you, and I still have time to serve God. The good news is my legs do relax after I move around and do some walking. My versatility is back. Versatility is just not for the body. It is also for the mind. Try to keep up with me; be as versatile in your ways as I am with my ways. I can do something, and for some reason, it just doesn't seem to look like my plans. The good thing again, I can change it to satisfy me as I am versatile. Same works for you if you fall in love. Everything seems to be fine and wonderful in the beginning. You think in your mind, "This is so wonderful. I finally met the right one." That's a good thing, but as you get to know the one you thought was your one and only, he didn't turn out the way you dreamed about. Again, you are versatile, and you have the versatility to say, "Sorry, I don't think this working out," and you move on. (*Don't forget to thank Jesus for this awakening.*) Final thoughts about versatility: You should never be versatile with our God. Always believe in God and his son Jesus. Do not believe in them, and when things seems to go awry, you do not believe in them. Being versatile shouldn't even enter your mind. God gave you the right to be versatile with all things. Never change your mind about God and his son Jesus. Thank you, Jesus.

Voices

At one time or another, we think we hear voices, and there is no one around but us. No, we are not going insane. I think the voice we hear is God trying to get our attention. He does that only if and when we need him. He does that when Satan is trying to influence you to do something wrong, which is against him. "God." It is wise to think of God or his son Jesus when you are troubled. Do not dwell on the voices, but just pay attention to your conscience. You are a strong person, and God will never steer you down a path you would rather not go; just pay attention to that voice and not the voice of Satan, who is trying to win you over. Trust yourself to overcome the evil thoughts, and you will remain free. Free from doing the wrong thing. When you remain free, your smile will be natural; it will be a medicine for your soul. If it is a sin you think you committed, ask for forgiveness and move on. Again, I must stress, do not dwell on those voices as they will go away when you want them to; thus, freedom again for you as now you are without sin. Thanks to Jesus and our will to listen to his voice.

Don't be afraid of life.
My life is a story yet to be told.
When stray thoughts arrive, stay the course.

Wanted

We have to think about this word and what it means as it has so many meanings to think about. Where do we start? Let's try the beginning as that sometimes seems to work a lot better. There is something or some things that I saw that I want. I'm not sure I need those things, but I wanted them. Am I lost and don't know where to turn to? I want advice on my dilemma. Please, if you know the answer, can you give me what I want? I wanted children, and God gave me what I wanted. A family. Someone made a mistake and broke man's law, so now they're wanted. So sad. Satan had his eyes on everyone for a very long time. I'm sure he has his followers. So why does he want me? He should go about his business and stop wanting me. I sure don't want him. What I wanted was peace of mind and someone to love me and only me. God gave me what I wanted, a loving wife and wonderful children. I wanted to be a part of God's life as long as I could remember. I wanted many material things that God did not give me, and now I realize why God didn't. It was for my own good that I did not get what I wanted. So I say to you, think wisely about the things you want now and the things you wanted in the past. And thank God and his son Jesus for giving you the wisdom to choose what you want.

Why is the best part saved for last?
A story is as short or as long as you want it to be.

Who Is Abaddon?

Abaddon may be in charge of you after death, depending on how terrible you are in life. If you lived your life as an atheist and did not believe in God, you fit in this category. If you are just plain mean, you fit in this category. If you hate the world, you fit in this category. If you show no remorse for your actions, you fit in this category. If you despise your fellow man, you fit in this category. I could go on and on, but I'm positive you *do not understand* as to *who Abaddon is*. He is your *punishment on Earth*, and you will be placed under him as a fallen angel after death with no chance of returning to your loved ones, a choice you made, not God; it's too bad you can't understand this while you are living. You may have had a better life in time to come. Under him, you would wish Satan claimed you; you are now among the fallen angels and a world with only despair. I guess maybe that is what you may already be used to.

Now is better than never.

Why

We hear people say certain things on the Internet, and we repeat what they say. In other words, we post what others say. To me, it's fascinating to pass on the good things said and to post them on your site so your friends can enjoy the saying that was posted. What I don't understand is why friends and relatives do not post your accomplishments—probably too close to home. So sad. I am proud of my family, and I do repeat the good things but leave out the bad things to make them more important or at least important enough to help them. Family members should be aware of the talent in their family. They should post what that member accomplished and post his or her accomplishments as they do a stranger's, and do all they can to help that family member achieve his or her goals. In some cases, the right person will see your post and also help with your goals. Alas, they do not—so sad. So I guess I will wait to become famous on my own without their help.

Yes

When I look in the mirror, I want to see the man I was forty years ago. But what I see is that man is long gone. His heart and mind are the same—maybe even better. Yes, that day will come for all of us who live beyond our years. I say "beyond our years" because I see most of my acquaintances pass away. No, I am not afraid of the word die or death; I just want to put that thought in the back of my mind—shelve it for now. I also don't dwell on the past, as there are some things in my life I would like to leave in the past. Only myself and God know those things, and we will discuss them down the road.

Speaking of roads, some of the paths I traveled were not the paths I would normally take, but nonetheless, I did travel those paths, and yes, I will own them. Most of the time, I wished I had come to a crossroads and taken another path, but those crossroads were sometimes so far away. But they did come, and I did take the path God chose. Just to clarify my past: those bad roads were a nuisance and a waste of time, but nothing to keep me out of heaven.

And yes, I am telling all you young people—don't lose sight of your true goals in life. Those goals should be to make your parents and God proud. And also, in the process, make yourself proud.

Even if your curiosity gets the best of you, don't go there.
(Jerry Manukin, 08-20-2024)

Within the pages of this journal, you will
find peace and happiness and love.

These are the words given to me spiritually through Simon Peter.

This book is the Bible of life.

1. If I knew then what I know now, I still wouldn't know.
2. Why is the best part saved for last?
3. If I had (wanted) a friend, it would be you.
4. You should handle the little things.
5. So you think you have a busy day.
6. We all have open wounds.
7. You should heal those wounds.
8. Let me help carry that burden.
9. If it's not good on this hand, why is it good on the other hand?
10. There are many steps to heal a crisis, but the first step is yours.
11. Why do you ask for a pair of scissors when you only need one?
12. My goal is to make me happy.
13. Excluding age, when does a child become an adult?
14. Don't worry. *God will find you.*
15. My goals are now yours.
16. Don' t put off praying and giving thanks.
17. Let children be children, but at your pace.
18. Sometimes now may not be until tomorrow.
19. If yesterday is today, when is tomorrow?
20. Happiness is contagious and so is sorrow.
21. Pick a time when you want your life to begin.
22. Pay attention when I'm talking to you.
23. Some people need a heater in their heart.
24. I don't understand because I'm not part of your world.
25. Don't be afraid to say I'm proud of you.
26. Imaginary pain hurts as bad as physical pain.
27. If not for the bad things, how would we know the good things?
28. Sometimes I try to remember to forget.
29. Sometimes you should interrupt right before you hear the word *but.*

30.   You can live your normal life and still love God.
31.   You don't have to be on your knees to pray.
32.   Not only can I lead a horse to water, but I can also make him drink.
33.   You never worry about pushing your luck when you have Jesus.
34.   I have my own personal rain cloud.
35.   I would like to believe I'm living in my world.
36.   I have enough time to live. I don't have to borrow any.
37.   Does a person of eighty years have lesser value than a twenty-one-year-old?
38.   You're the problem. Jesus is the solution.
39.   If you reach out, my hand will be there.
40.   A goodbye kiss is only once.
41.   Sometimes I think I'm behind when actually I'm way ahead.
42.   Somebody does know your thoughts.
43.   Sometimes fantasy is better than reality.
44.   There is no answer to why.
45.   Because is never an answer.
46.   Too many thoughts are wasted on a friendship.
47.   I love it when we work together separately.
48.   I can't tell you more than I know.
49.   You're me, and I'm you.
50.   Skip the sarcasm and just pretend to be friends.
51.   When stray thoughts arrive, stay the course.
52.   The fire within you is Satan, and Jesus is the fireman.
53.   I do not wish to be your friend, nor do I wish to be your enemy.
54.   If you're desperate for a friend, Jesus is available.
55.   Sometimes the impossible is impossible.
56.   Even bad things come to an end.
57.   I long to hear the sound of violins.
58.   A few meaningless words can fill a huge book.
59.   You are the building.
60.   I'm listening.

61. You may not realize the person standing next to you may be your guardian angel.
62. Always be glad that you are you.
63. My life is a story yet to be told.
64. I would like to believe in my world the sun is always shining.
65. Don't be afraid of life.
66. The truth can only be told one way.
67. A lie has many avenues.
68. A story is as short or as long as you want it to be.
69. Life has no reverse.
70. Each saying has a story behind it.
71. Why is there more rain in some lives than others?
72. I can read minds if you don't scribble.
73. Best way to get someone to do something is to tell them not to do it.
74. It's hard to make ends meet when you're going around in circles.
75. Start today if you want to get to tomorrow.
76. You don't have to go the extra mile for me, a couple of feet will do.
77. What is what?
78. In God's world, how high would you climb that mountain?
79. I believe in God; also I believe in me.
80. You must follow God and lead others.
81. Jesus understands my life.
82. As of now, I'm still human.
83. When we do something we are not sure of, make sure it's God's thing, not Satan's.
84. You must fear God, not because of him but because of you.
85. I will never cast the first stone.
86. I don't understand the Bible, but I do understand God and life.
87. In the past, *reasonable* was the word.
88. In the present, *confusion* is the word.

89. Tomorrow is here.

90. This is not what I do; this is what I did.

91. What I learn from these times is that some geniuses are idiots.

92. Physical and mental pain only hurts when you think about it.

93. You should never feel guilty about good things.

94. Instead of putting up with Satan, evict him from your mind.

95. You must feel good enough about yourself to believe prayer works.

96. Some people are free, and they still feel unfree.

97. Analyze this.

98. Don't wait for something that's not there.

99. I don't want people to know I exist.

100. It's time for you to hear me.

101. I have talked the talk, but I never walked the walk.

102. I will fight the battles within me.

103. You don't have to shout for God to hear you.

104. His messages are clear.

105. Why do you accept the words of others when his words are clear?

106. I am the last to be recognized.

107. I have seen miracles.

108. I can't wait for tomorrow.

109. The grass always looks greener on the other side; remember, it's not your grass.

110. Focus on what blessings you had, not the ones you want.

111. The things I try to remember I forget.

112. The things I try to forget I remember.

113. How can you not believe?

114. Don't wish for a miracle; wish for miracles.

115. When you're at heaven's gate, make sure it says "enter" not "exit."

116. New day, same life, better outlook.

117. When you tell people you trust them, make sure your fingers are crossed.
118. I would gladly meet you halfway if I knew where to start.
119. If you already know, why are you asking me?
120. Silence is deafening.
121. I can't be quiet; I already have a name.
122. Some people should not act naturally.
123. Love yourself so you may love others.
124. The best secrets are the ones yet to be told.
125. Life is real; dreams are not.
126. If not removed, the chip you have on your shoulder may become a log.
127. God knows you. Do you know you?
128. Sometimes getting a little crazy is good for the soul.
129. I have no more cheeks to turn.
130. If you think you're not you, look in the mirror.
131. No, you can't see through me.
132. Who are they?
133. Be alert; reality is just around the corner.
134. My wife picked the second choice in our vowels.
135. You can get there from here.
136. Make sure the voice you hear is God's.
137. Don't pay someone a compliment and then take it back.
138. There are polite ways to offend someone.
139. Have you lost weight? Your mouth used to be bigger.
140. I want to be happy.
141. Yes, God knows you.
142. I'm in love with me.
143. I will always put God first.
144. I'm glad to be second.
145. Hypocrisy, yes, it is you, not me.
146. I bring good luck to bad people.
147. I know two things, and I just told you one.
148. Satan has my mouth, but Jesus has my heart.
149. This day will end with or without me.
150. Money doesn't talk; it shouts.

151. It's harder to be good than be bad.
152. You have to work at being good.
153. Being bad takes no effort.
154. If you want to be right half of the time, pick the second choice.
155. Let my faults be limited and protect me and all that is close to me.
156. If you have no cents you will never be a millionaire.
157. I don't want to sneeze before you bless me.
158. The way the world is heading today, Satan may not have a job.
159. Time is on your side; mine is limited.
160. Satan is temporary; Jesus is forever.
161. Why are you afraid to ask for help?
162. I don't want to have the last laugh.
163. Sometimes, the things I think about are not my thoughts.
164. Jesus is not only a way out but a way in.
165. If I gave you a piece of my mind, I wouldn't have any left.
166. God is the medicine for your soul.
167. I don't want to walk a mile in your shoes.
168. Don't lose sight of you; reality is right around the corner.
169. Emotion lets you know you have a heart.
170. In order to get close to someone, you may need to back off.
171. The rosary is your most valuable possession.
172. I can give you what I don't have because I'm not using it anyway.
173. I may lose, but I am not a loser.
174. What maybe is, or maybe it's not.
175. Is it possible to be alone with someone?
176. God is the foundation; you are the building.
177. I have two: one I pray to and the other I pray for.
178. Please leave my world alone.
179. Being honorable and loving and righteous makes for a good night of sleep and pretty dreams.
180. Who are they?

181. Don't drive yourself crazy; let a friend do it.
182. God's favorite numbers are seven and forty.
183. It works for all that is pure of the heart.
184. Now is better than never.
185. Now and forever.

1940 to forever.

In Closing

If Jesus gave me three wishes, the first I would give to all of you so you may have a wish. The second wish I would give to my wife Judith, son Jerry, and daughter Michele. And the third and final, I would give back to Jesus to give to his Father and thank him for being so proud of his son and his adopted children, as I am of my family.

Thank you.

Family Tree

I am just a branch on my family tree. This tree is for my relatives and their familys. If I were to go back in time my family tree's would be a forrest. So lets not complicate things and talk about the family members on my family tree in this life.(My life) how many times have we heard someone say (about a loved one, whether it be wife or husband or mother and father or a sister or brother or just a loved one) I will be with them in heaven. (Not taking away from your beliefs) but your loved ones are and should be only a memory. Because I believe they (their soul) is about to continue their life on another family tree. Don't be sad, it is a good thing the way God sets up family trees. If you want to help a deceased relative on your family tree pray to God and ask him to send a guardian angel from heaven to whom ever you want (you should say their names) for them to have a blessing in their new life. Love and life is an eternity. Life has a beginning but has no end even after death. As an example if you lost a loved one three years ago that person(soul) is now three years old in their new life once they return to earth. Remember how much time you spend and praise God and help prople to be Christian, you may stay and enjoy heaven for some time. After that is when the years start, right after you return to your new life.

Jerry Manukin

Hate and Love

Lets start with hate, the H in hate means pure <u>hell</u> in your life. You dislike everyone. You have no feelings at all for anyone. Next lets take the A in hate. The A in hate means you have a bad <u>attitude</u>. You (<u>when I say you it could mean anyone, not necessarily you, or maybe it is you</u>), you speak down on everyone like you are the greatest. Next lets take the T in hate. The T means temper. You cannot remain calm like most people should. You seem to go extreme when you dislike what others say or do. Finally lets take the E in hate. The E in hate means <u>enough</u> of this. Lets cut out this nonsense and move our mind and body to love.

Lets get to the word love. (<u>I am feeling better now that hate is out of the way and out of me</u>) the L in love means I am <u>looking good</u>. Feeling good, pleasant to be around people and myself. <u>The</u> O in hate means <u>offer</u>. I will offer you some thing to make you smile, maybe I may tell you a funny joke or simply tell you a happy story. The V in love means <u>victory</u>. You have defeated your evil and unwanted thoughts. You are now so proud of yourself. The E in love means <u>energy</u>. You now have the spirit to do things, not because you have to, but because you want to. You have the energy to move around being proud of yourself for the happiness you bring to others. Now that we know the difference between hate and love. Hate is an ugly word and love is as it sounds. When you say I hate you, the smile you had went away. Both parties were sad. When you say I love you to someone, the smile appears on both parties, there is happiness in your life and theirs. Both parties are now happy.

Love you, Jerry Manukin

I Remember

As I lay here all my thoughts are about me and my loved ones. I don't wish to be a burden or a hardship for any of my family. You must remember those are your thoughts and not theirs. They don't mind taking care of you as you cared for them when they were younger. When you were young you was full of life and vinegar, as the saying goes. Hold on to that thought while you are recovering. Take the recovery time as a blessing. Control where your mind goes. Maybe I can help. Lets think about your years when you loved to hunt and fish, and still do. How nice and spirit lifting was the thrill of the hunt and the bragging about the big one (the fish that got away). Also when I recover I will thank God for the wisdom and strenght he gave to me during my recovery. Also I am not forgetting to thank my loved ones. They were the ones who kept me strong with their love for me. I honestly believe I had repaid for all the wrong you and I thought I did in all my years. And just to satisfy myself I will confess all my sins directly to God. And then I know I am covered. Also thank you Jesus for putting a good word in to your father for me, telling him I am a good man.

Jerry Manukin
05-27-2024

Mother's Day Memories

Here we go again, another mother's day, just another day. Not so, I remember when it started with the two of us. I was wondering what my life would be like, well that was short lived, because I just created a masterpiece with my first child. And another masterpiece with my second child. The pain of having children was well worth it, and I was rewarded many times over when I first heard the word mommy. That one word(mommy) was heard with my ears and felt with my heart. I never got tired or frustrated when I would hear mommy fifteen or more times a day. It was a magical feeling. Now the mommy is no more, now it is mom. And not fifteen times a day or more. But it pleasured me when I did hear it. Now the time is when I hear my children say mother. My memories brings a tear to my eyes especialy when one or the other slips and calls me mommy. Those were the good old days. Now as it was in the beginning is now full circle. Now I hope some day my daughter has the same memories as I have.

"Your loving husband Jerry"

Realization of Life

Some people feel like they have a weight on there shoulders. That weight could be just your thoughts or just simply the way you choose to live. That's one side of the coin, the other side is carrying a chip on your shoulder. How heavy or lite that weight or chip on your shoulder depends on you. No one else is to blame. Lets take chip's for instance, chip's are your attitude. The longer we leave that chip there it can began to grow. Nonsence you say, well we will see. Chips are like stair cases, one step, small chip, 2 steps a branch, 3 steps a trunk, 4 steps a limb, 5 steps a tree-which becomes a log on your shoulder. You should chip away at that attitude, whoops I mean log until it is a chip again. And then you can brush away that attitude (chip) with one stroke of your hand. You hear people say all of the time when a problem or crisis arises and then goes away, boy it feels like a giant weight has been removed. So true after that weight/chip/attitude has been lifted thank our God and keep the faith. Now we have a clearer view of our lives. Don't make whatever happened ever happen again. A small sacrifice to make for a healthier life. You can go to a dictionary to look up things you want to know or you can just ask Jesus for answers as he know more than a dictionary and the good part is there are not hundreds of pages to search through for answers just look into your heart.

Jerry Manukin

Recovering Alcoholic

After the fact is when the bravery the strength and mostly the believing in our God kicks in. It should have kicked in before this dilemma, it didn't so lets move on. You wasted many years of your life(and possible other lives as well) lets start with the ones who were addicted to alcohol for lets say 4 years or less. Well. If you realized that you were an alcoholic in that short period of time you should feel lucky you realized it in that short of time. None the less those were hell years, mentally and physically.(again not to mention hell for your loved ones too) when I said you were lucky this is what I meant. Some went on to be alcoholics for 26years or more and possibly their whole lives. So sad, as a lifetime was lost, that's bad enough but what about the Dui's and the unpaid bills and the things your husband/wife/children went thru and finally the divorce you went through. Lets hope your alcoholizm did not make you abusive. I do have two questions for you. One is why did you start to drink? And the other is what made you decide to quit? I'm sure those questions entered your mind, I'm sure you had many a sleepless nite trying to answer those two questions especially the first one. So, now you are on the path to righteousness. Your memory start to come back and your health is improving. But you are still going thru hell, but after some time this hell will go away the other would not. You have lost a lot over this experience and if you ever feel the urge to take a drink, don't. God believes you have the strength and so do I. Remember now it is about you and you alone. Now that your recovering and stay recovered you will have a place in heaven, that is God's reward to you.

Jerry Manukin 05-27-2024

Trapped

Why do the majority of us feel trapped? We may not even know it. We may just be spinning our wheels, and going nowhere. Trapped. We may be trapped in our failures in life or we may be trapped in our sucesses in life. Never the less we are trapped. Let me try to explain what I mean by being trapped. We go through our daily routines as if we have nothing else to do, we just do. I think maybe that is where the saying stop and smell the roses comes from. We would like to, but we just don't have enough time in the day. Let me tell you straight up, make the time. Do something you want to not because you have to, but because you feel like it. Learn to enjoy life, don't fall into the many traps in all of our lives. Remember you are not alone. There are millions like you. Trapped. Lets free ourselves from this bondage. How you say, well let me tell you, start with a little prayer for yourself, don't know any prayers, well now you know why you feel trapped. Any one can say a prayer, just use your own words, God doesn't want you to be formal. He just wants to know you care. He wants you to be free. Free from your thoughts and deeds. Freedom is there just for the asking. Cost no money to be free. Just love. Start with yourself, you must love yourself before you can love others. In a short time after your mindset has changed you will start to feel free. You are no longer trapped in life. Don't waste time with your new found freedom, enjoy life, and enjoy the favors God will bestow upon you.

Jerry Manukin
07-01-2024

Until we Meet Again

This is a message of hope for the ones who truly had a soul mate in this life and one or the other had passed away, again don't be sad because God looks after you and your loved ones in this life and the next life. Remember when I said on your family tree this is your life now, and let your loved one be a memory. Well the hope is you may meet the one you lost in this new life after death. Try not to be confused with what I'm saying. I'm trying to tell you, you may be friends with your lost loved one in this new life and you both may end up on another family tree together in this new life. You may even re-marry in this life. Don't rush to make a new life for yourself as you can do more in this life for your lost loved one. Remember again pray for your lost love and don't forget to have God look after them, as you and them know how many times you thought you wished you had a guardian angel, well nows your chance to give them a guardian angel so they may have many blessings and some one to protect them in their new life.

Jerry Manukin

About the Author

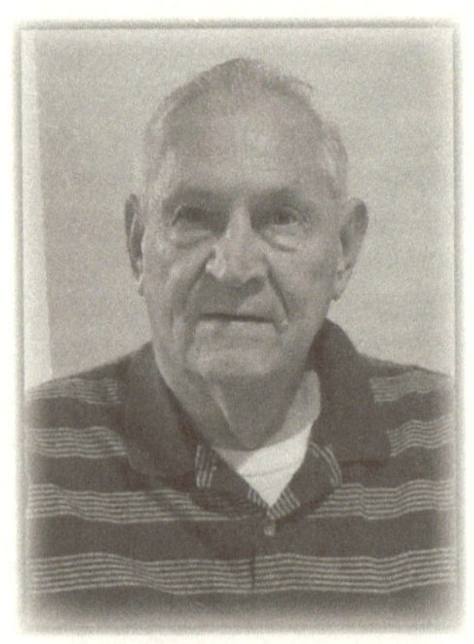

Jerry was born on a hillside in Blaine, Ohio, in June of 1940. He graduated high school and married at age twenty-three. He has two adult children. He also owns and operates a ten-lane bowling center for sixty-two years, and even as a child, he believed in God. Throughout his teens, he would try to make others understand God, especially by his actions, as he would never push his religion on others because he believes in God for all. As he got older, he began to research the saints to see which one he closely followed, and as he got to Simon Peter, he thought he was looking at his life; and the letters he wrote he felt came from him spiritually.